S0-ASO-313

The HUNTER'S BOOK OF THE

ELK

NORTH·AMERICAN·HUNTING·CLUB

The HUNTER'S BOOK OF THE ELK

Text by JOHN BARSNESS

Photography by MICHAEL FRANCIS

ABOUT THE AUTHOR

John Barsness started elk hunting at age 12, the first autumn he legally could, and in the years since has hunted them with bow and rifle from Idaho to New Mexico. Educated in wildlife biology at the University of Montana, his articles on the outdoors have appeared in more than 40 magazines, including *National Geographic, Outdoor Life* and *Sports Illustrated*. He currently writes regularly for eight magazines, including *American Hunter, Field & Stream* and *Gray's Sporting Journal*, and he's the author of six previous books, including *The Life Of The Hunt*, an award-winning collection of big game hunting stories. He lives in southwestern Montana with his wife, the writer and photographer Eileen Clarke, two Labrador retrievers and thousands of elk.

ABOUT THE PHOTOGRAPHER

Michael H. Francis, born in Maine, has spent the past thirty years as a resident of Montana. Mike is a graduate of Montana State University. Previous to becoming a full-time photographer, he worked seasonally in Yellowstone National Park for 15 years. Mike's photography has been internationally recognized for its beautiful and informative nature imagery. His work has been published by the *National Geographic Society*, the *Audubon Society*, the *National Wildlife Federation*, and *Field & Stream, Outdoor Life* and *North American Hunter* magazines, among others. He has photographed more than 15 books including: *The Hunter's Book of the Whitetail; Track of the Coyote; Mule Deer Country; Elk Country; Wild Sheep Country* and *Moose*. Mike lives in Billings, Montana, with his family.

The HUNTER'S BOOK of THE ELK

Printed in 2012.

9 10 11 12 / 15 14 13 12
ISBN 10: 1-58159-126-8
ISBN 13: 978-1-58159-126-2
© 2001 North American Hunting Club

North American Hunting Club
12301 Whitewater Drive
Minnetonka, MN 55343
www.huntingclub.com

TOM CARPENTER
Creative Director

HEATHER KOSHIOL
Senior Book Development Coordinator

SHARI GROSS
Senior Book Development Assistant

SUSAN KANEKO BINKLEY
Book Design and Production

DAN KENNEDY
Photo Editor

PHOTO CREDITS
All photos © **Michael H. Francis** except the following: **Phil Aarrestad,** 30; **Donald M. Jones,** 1, 16–17, 40, 50, 57, 64, 108, 137; **Lee Kline,** 61, 70–71, 74–75, 83, 142, 172; **Leonard Rue Enterprises,** 27; **Gary Leppart,** 4 (bottom); **NAHC,** 60; **Dusan Smetana/The Green Agency,** 138; **Tom Teitz,** 5, 47, 113, 150, 178, 183, 186.

Table of Contents

Introduction

ORIGINS, HISTORY AND MYTHS

THE ELK & NORTH AMERICA

Look—down there in the dawn meadow—a bull elk, flanks burnt-orange against yellow grass, breath-smoke rising from his nostrils. He's easily a half-mile away, but through our 8X glasses we can see the firefly-gleam of the dozen white points along the walnut-brown beams of his antlers. He tilts his head, and steam erupts from his mouth as from a cold volcano; two adrenaline-quick heartbeats later we hear his hoarse whistle rise toward the brassy sky and then fade into the lodgepole pine along the meadow's edge. We don't say anything, but agree silently that there, in the September dawn, stands the finest wild animal we have ever seen.

—John Barsness

According to wildlife biologists, North American elk are one of the most highly evolved deer on earth. "Highly evolved" in biology-speak does not mean what it might mean to you or me or anybody else eavesdropping on a September bull. Evolutionary science does not rank life-forms in the same way we list college football teams or best-selling diet books, implying that one animal is "better" than another. Instead, "highly evolved" means that elk have evolved—changed—more from their ancestors than most other deer that have survived until the 21st century. (Then again, that doesn't mean elk are not the finest animals in North America, at least according to many humans who still revere the truly wild.)

Deer have lived on our planet for about 35 million years. "Old World" deer (as opposed to American "New World" deer such as mule and white-tailed deer) originated in the tropics but soon spread to dry grasslands, temperate forests, alpine mountains

A bull elk sends his September song into the mountains. Elk are the largest of the "red deer," a family that stretches around the globe from the British Isles to North America.

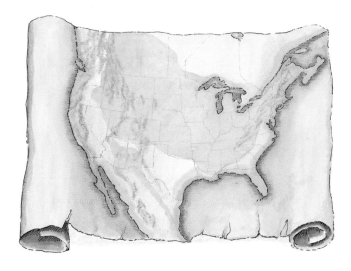

and even the arctic. Life in the tropics differs from all those other environments: There's a lot of food and leafy cover available year-round. So the original deer tended to be small and slithery (to avoid predators), and had tusks to defend their little piece of cover and food from other deer. They only had small antlers, or none at all, because antlers are not really weapons—at least not like tusks.

As Old World deer spread across the planet, they retained two of their ancestors' early characteristics: shrunken tusks and a preference for relatively soft food, like the ever-growing plants of the tropics. Unlike elephants and other "super ruminants," deer cannot survive long on old, tough vegetation, whether it's grasses or twigs. Tender new growth occurs on what biologists call new environments, land that's been scraped clean by fire, glaciers, flood, drought or overgrazing by other animals.

Our elk belong to a family of deer that exists from the

Though elk are being transplanted to many areas these days, they are primarily Western mountain animals.

Before Europeans settled in North America, elk inhabited much of the continent.

British Isles across Europe and Asia to the southwestern United States, a family loosely called red deer. The red deer of Europe (*Cervus elaphus*) were the first of this family to be classified in Linnaen nomenclature by Swedish biologist Carl von Linne, almost 250 years ago. Human culture, for better or worse, has often evolved from Europe. When English settlers first arrived in what's known as New England, they found very large deer they called "elk," because they had heard of but had never seen the large "elk" of Europe—the animals we know as "moose."

Those first English-speaking Europeans eventually found moose only in the northern half of the continent, but back then, elk almost covered the New World. With the exception of Florida and northern New England, elk existed in every one of today's contiguous 48 states, northern Mexico, and every southern province of Canada from Quebec to British Columbia.

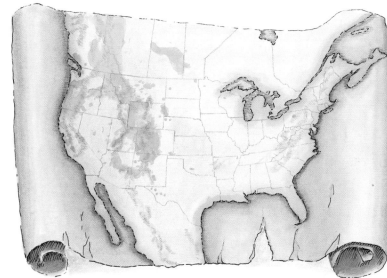

*T*hough there are a few earlier traces of each species, as the last Ice Age started to wind down some 12,000 to 13,000 years ago, signs of both humans and elk began showing up over much of North America.

Some of the earliest archaeological sites that show evidence of Indians preying on elk are in Alaska, where elk bones have been found mixed with the bones of other prehistoric grazers such as horses, mountain sheep, bison and caribou. Except for horses (which evolved on this continent), all these species, including humans, first arrived in North America via the Bering land bridge. That bridge was only crossable when much of the earth's water was locked up in Ice Age glaciers, so it's natural that some of the elk's earliest traces should be found in Alaska.

But both elk and people spread rapidly. An archaeological site in Wyoming, from the early Folsom culture (carbon dating to about 10,500 years ago, soon after the glacial ice melted), has parts of elk antlers mixed with human debris. One piece found was a brow tine cut from the base of an antler, used as a tool for chipping the long "flute" on the sides of typical Folsom spear points.

But after that, elk are relatively rare in archaeological sites in the West. Not that they weren't "utilized," as archaeologists put it. But after the weather warmed and the glaciers receded, the coniferous forests that covered large parts of North America also receded, becoming the vast grasslands known as the Great Plains. Here bison dominated the large herbivores and so, over the next few thousand years, many Native Americans adapted into the bison culture that eventually culminated in the horse-riding tribes—after Europeans brought back the descendants of the now-extinct North American horse.

But elk did mix into the Plains Indian culture, especially in the last thousand years, as evidenced by remains found in widespread archaeological sites. And elk "ivory" teeth were almost as valued by several Plains tribes as by the Benevolent and Protective Order of Elks. Buckskin shirts and dresses almost covered with elk teeth still exist in museums today, and one anthropologist noted that to many tribes, one elk-tooth dress was worth two good buffalo horses. Farther south, elk bones have been found in sites in northern Arizona and New Mexico dating as far back as 12,000 years.

Elk were hunted more by Native Americans in the Pacific Northwest and Midwest, in areas where buffalo were never abundant if they existed at all. In sites from northern California up through Washington and British Columbia, hundreds of elk-antler tools have been found, including scrapers for curing hides, war clubs, digging sticks and adze handles. Many sites in the Ohio River Valley and Great Lakes region contain elk bones, and some archaeologists see elk shapes in many of the mounds built by Native Americans in the Ohio, Illinois and Wisconsin regions.

Elk bones never show up abundantly in Native American sites in the East, where they're vastly outnumbered by the bones of white-tailed deer. But northeastern Native Americans did hunt elk, and also fished frequently in the abundant rivers and lakes, often making barbed harpoon-tips out of elk tines.

Continued . . .

Continued from page 13

Most elk bones found in archaeological sites are dated to less than 5,000 years ago, and it's doubtful that Native Americans ever harmed elk populations much; there simply weren't enough people/hunters. Population estimates vary, but all the evidence indicates that only a few million Native Americans ever existed at any one time. Their biggest influence on elk populations may have been positive, especially in recent centuries. There's ample evidence, mostly from historical times, that Native Americans often deliberately set fire to timber and grassland to promote new vegetative growth that would attract wild game.

Burning may have been more frequent after they acquired horses, allowing more mobility. Then Native Americans could burn an area near where they lived, then move near a slightly older burn for a few years until the new burn grew into prime elk and deer food.

Horse tribes on the plains also sometimes drove elk over cliffs just as they did buffalo, and even occasionally "ran" elk, riding alongside the fleeing animals and shooting them with arrows or guns at close range. One Plains tribe, the Sarsi, even reportedly decoyed elk into impoundments, where they were slaughtered with spears, knives and clubs.

Native American elk hunting ran the gamut of all the common traditional techniques. In various parts of the country, hunters used snares and deadfalls, made drives (especially into impoundments), took stands near trails or mineral licks, or hunted elk on snowshoes in deep snow. George Bird Grinnell reported that Eastern tribes hung a rawhide noose from a string branch over elk trails, and similar reports came from settlers in California. When a passing elk caught its head in the noose, it panicked and strangled itself. Dogs were sometimes used, especially before the horse, to drive elk toward snares or impoundments.

Some tribes built deep pits along elk trails, especially in heavily forested regions. Early explorers in the Pacific Northwest, including Lewis and Clark and Jedediah Smith, reported that several tribes used this technique quite effectively, sometimes placing sharpened stakes at the bottom of the pit to kill or disable the elk. Other Northwestern tribes placed nets across trails and drove herds of elk into them, tangling their legs and heads in the nets.

Near lakes or ocean bays, Native Americans often drove elk into water, or intercepted them as they naturally swam from land to land, killing them from canoes with clubs, spears or arrows.

And some Natives, of course, were adept still-hunters, able to sneak close enough to kill elk with both bow and spear. After they acquired horses, Plains Indians typically wintered not out on the open prairie but in canyons along the edge of the mountains, and used their steeds to hunt elk on winter range. Elmer Keith, the late hunting writer, grew up in Montana in the early part of the century, and reported that Flathead Indians still made communal pack trips of dozens of miles to hunt elk in the valleys surrounding their land. Horses made it much easier to pack large chunks of meat long distances.

Modern hunters regard elk meat as among the finest-tasting wild game, and revere its low fat content, which supposedly makes it much healthier than higher-fat domestic meats. But there's evidence, both incidental and historical, that Native Americans didn't think elk meat was all that special.

Plains tribes preferred fat buffalo, some finding elk "unpalatably sweet," like white man's beef, a choice echoed in the journals of most white fur trappers. Having eaten both prime elk and buffalo, I vote buffalo too. Meat from a cow or young bull elk is very good, but no better than prime whitetail, bighorn sheep or even mule deer. Here it must also be noted that Native

Americans did not just eat the carcass meat from an elk, but the tongue, innards and even the blood.

They did prefer certain parts of an elk, and numerous tribes ranked them in this order: flank and backstrap, hindquarters, ribs, innards, brisket and front quarters. (I can personally attest that elk ribs are far more edible than deer ribs, mostly because the fat doesn't congeal as easily.) The long bones were broken for marrow, and in some tribes, unborn calves were considered particularly tasty.

Elk, unlike buffalo, were usually eaten fresh, rather than made into pemmican or jerky (though it was often used there too). This is because elk were usually hunted only when buffalo weren't around, and also because fatter buffalo meat kept body and soul together better during a cold winter, when dried meat and jerky were most often eaten. Because it was leaner, elk was usually cooked more gently than buffalo, usually by boiling. Overcooking tends to toughen lean meat more than fat meat.

But part of the preference for buffalo, I suspect, was sheer availability. Buffalo lived on the plains year-round, while elk (that supposed "plains" animal), usually stayed off the wide-open plains unless forced there by fire, insects or weather. Elk could run, hide and climb steep hills

far better than buffalo, so were harder to hunt.

Elk may have actually been hunted more for their hides, especially by Plains Indians. Not that the meat was abandoned, but many Plains tribes concentrated on hunting elk during summer, when the hides (particularly of cows and calves) were soft and most easily tanned. Elk leather, as anybody who's owned a pair of elk gloves can attest, is very thick and durable, and was especially used for moccasins or even battle shirts. Elk rawhide evidently could turn stone-tipped arrows. But even the more pliable hides of elk cows and calves were not often used for any but ceremonial clothing; thinner deer and buffalo skins were preferred for everyday wear.

Plains Natives used buffalo hides for sleeping robes, not bull elk hides, though a tanned, de-haired elk hide was often used as a summer robe, especially among Woodland Natives who didn't often kill buffalo. Some elk hides were used for shelter, especially when traveling, much like small tarpaulins. Elk skin was evidently more water resistant than other leathers; Lewis and Clark preferred it for keeping their gear dry. Some tepee covers were also made of elk, using anywhere from 6 to 20 hides sewn together. Many tribes

also used elk skin for covering boats or for rope, or for dozens of other everyday objects like bags and arrow quivers.

Hides also were important in trade and barter. Native American trade routes often covered more than a thousand miles; seashell beads from the Pacific Northwest have been found in the Midwest, and Yellowstone Park obsidian, that prime arrow-point stone, has been found all over the West. A durable leather-like elk hide must have been very valuable in trade with Native Americans in regions where elk were scarce. While not quite the all-around supermarket that the buffalo were to the Plains Indians, or that the white-tailed deer were to Eastern tribes, elk were eaten, worn, and transformed into tools, money and even ceremonies by every Native American tribe that lived in elk country.

PLAINS ANIMALS?

You may have read that elk were originally plains animals that eventually were driven into the mountains by the advance of what we call "civilization." I suspect this folktale originated with the journals of the Corps of Discovery, commonly known as the Lewis and Clark Expedition, the first contingent of white men to see much of what is today the high plains and northwestern mountains of the United States.

Lewis and Clark's men—and their female guide Sacajawea—ate lots of elk while they traveled the Great Plains via the Missouri River. But the group almost starved while crossing the mountains, seeing only a few deer and no elk. Some naturalists took this to mean that before the coming of Europeans, elk lived on the plains and not in the high mountains.

Lewis and Clark crossed the Rockies on Lolo Pass, on the present-day border of Montana and Idaho. In the 1800s, Lolo Pass was the most popular route used by the abundant Nez Percé of Idaho and Washington for traveling to the buffalo plains. The Nez Percé and other tribes crossed the pass whenever it wasn't covered with snow, and by September, when the Corps of Discovery crossed the mountains, almost all the limited grass along the route had been eaten by the Natives' horses, so no elk lived anywhere near the pass.

But elk lived elsewhere in the high Rockies. A fur trapper named Osborne Russell traveled the region 30 years after Lewis and Clark and, like the two captains, kept a journal of his travels. Late in September of 1837, near Yellowstone Lake in the middle of the mountains of present-day Yellowstone Park, Russell and his

Elk were not originally only plains animals. They thrive best in mixed terrain which includes grasslands, abundant water and timber thick enough to protect them from both summer heat and winter winds.

companions found "the whole country swarming with Elk." One night they were kept awake by the near-continuous bugling of rutting bulls. Other early journals of the beaver-trapping era tell similar tales.

Elk did disappear from the plains during the latter half of the 19th century, killed off by hungry miners, railroad workers and homesteaders, as well as commercial hunters who cut out tongues and pulled vestigial ivory tusks to sell to members of the Benevolent and Protective Order of Elks.

The last large herd of elk in the United States found refuge in Yellowstone Park, but they weren't driven there. Elk lived before that in the forests of the east, from New England to the Deep South. Were they driven onto the plains from New York and Tennessee? No, elk are not plains animals forced to live in the mountains. They were just killed off everywhere they could be killed easily, like most of the large game of the "howling wilderness" the Pilgrims found. Not strictly plains animals, elk are highly adaptable deer capable of living anywhere grassland mixes with timber, north of the Tropic of Cancer and south of the Canadian tundra.

oday elk are populating—or more precisely, in most cases, repopulating—areas where no elk existed in the 20th century. While hunting pronghorns in southwestern

DESERT ELK

New Mexico recently, several members of my party saw a cow elk on the flat desert south of Fort Sumner. And elk are also slowly spreading southward in Arizona. Meanwhile, in the northern deserts of eastern Montana and Wyoming, and even in the Dakotas, elk continue to populate new country.

Judging from what we know about their past history in North America, elk are obviously highly adaptable animals, but just how well will they adapt to desert living? Since they were already living there when Lewis and Clark went through, elk should do well in the northern deserts, like the Badlands and high short-grass plains of Montana, Wyoming and the western Dakotas. Good elk food is everywhere in that part of the country, so all they need is some thermal cover to cope with winter's minus 40°F temperatures.

But the southern deserts are something else. Most of the elk in Arizona and New Mexico live in high mountains, and mostly in the northern parts of both states. The weather around Flagstaff, Arizona, or Taos,

As elk populations continue to increase across the continent, they're expanding into areas not usually thought of as elk habitat, including deserts, both northern and southern. Here a cow stands alert in the badlands of North Dakota.

New Mexico, isn't all that different from the weather in southwestern Montana. But to adapt to the true lowland deserts in both states, elk will probably have to grow smaller.

Two biological rules will affect the elk that may adapt to true desert life. Bergmann's Rule postulates that body size increases the farther the animal lives from the equator. There are some obvious exceptions to Bergmann's Rule, which is why some wildlife biologists are today disputing it. For instance, caribou grow largest along the 60th parallel of latitude, growing smaller farther north, finally ending up as a "dwarf" form on the islands in the Arctic Ocean, known as Peary's caribou.

But caribou are strictly northern animals. Even at their most abundant they barely existed in the coldest contiguous American states such as Maine, Minnesota and Montana. Most mammals found from anywhere near the tropics to the edge of the tundra do follow Bergmann's Rule, and also Allen's Rule, which postu-

lates that mammals farther from the equator have smaller extremities. Both adaptations allow animals to live either in the extreme cold of the northern temperate zone or in the hot weather farther south. Big bodies (Bergmann) help retain heat during winter; so do short ears (Allen), since they don't radiate as much heat. Conversely, small bodies and big ears allow southern animals to rid their internal organs of excess heat.

We already see this in North American elk. The Tule elk of California live in the warmest climate of any elk, as citizens of the Central Valley can attest. Tule elk are much smaller than any of the other elk— adult bulls weigh about 550 pounds, as opposed to 750 to 800 pounds or the other races—and they tend to have larger heads and ears, often appearing nearly as front-heavy as caribou. Since elk have been truly established in North America for only about 11,000 years, this is a relatively quick adaptation to the California climate.

But many recent evolutionary studies (including work done with the finches of the Galapagos Islands, the very birds that helped formulate George Darwin's first book, *The Origin of Species,* suggest that adaptation to local conditions can happen much more quickly than scientists have long believed. The old concept that evolution took tiny steps over huge amounts of time is falling into disregard, one reason some biologists are beginning to believe that local differences in a species' size—or other superficial characteristics like color—are more due to quickly occurring physical adaptations than fundamental changes.

So the elk spreading southward in the Southwest may very soon be growing smaller. We may not see this change in the next 10 or 20 years, but if elk do become established in the southern desert, to our great-grandchildren they may end up looking much like the Tule elk of California.

THE NEW MEGAFAUNA

A friend of mine, a professional archaeologist who knows better but likes the sound of the phrase, says he likes to hunt elk because "they're the last of the Pleistocene megafauna." By this he means elk are one of the last large North American mammals left from the Ice Age that ended about 11,000 years ago, known as the Late Pleistocene Epoch or Ranchola-brean by paleontologists. ("Ranchola-brean" refers to the mix of animals found in the "tar pits" in the part of Los Angeles that used to be a cattle ranch known as Rancho La Brea.)

Though a few elk did show up in North America before the Late Pleistocene, they did not almost cover the continent until after the geologically recent "Wisconsin" glaciation, the last Ice Age, mentioned above. The true Pleistocene/Rancholabrean megafauna were animals such as "woolly" mammoths, giant sloths and the huge ancestor of the plains buffalo, *Bison latifrons*, whose horns often spread more than 6 feet. These giant grazers populated the plains, and large predators like saber-toothed "cats" (*Smilodon*) ate them.

These animals were much larger than most prehistoric mammals of the same era from Europe and Asia, because of the abundant predators that ate them. Under constant predation, prey species tend to grow larger, for two major reasons: Larger animals are harder to bring down, and fewer prey animals mean more food for those that survive. Sub-Saharan Africa is a perfect example, full of large predators and huge herbivores like elephants, rhinos, hippos, Cape buffalo and eland.

In theory, the Pleistocene megafauna rarely overgrazed their food source, unlike most European and Asian herbivores, which without the abundant predators of North America tended to have smaller bodies and larger teeth, the better to take advantage of any rough food available. We see this again and again when comparing related species from Europe and North America. Elk are much larger than red deer, just as American bison (*Bison bison*)—even the relatively small bison

---

Pre–Ice Age Pleistocene megafauna such as mammoths, giant sloths and huge bison had to die off before post-Pleistocene elk could populate most of North America.

of today—are bigger than the European wisent *(Bison bonasus)*. The exceptions all come from far northeastern Asia, which is essentially the same environment as far northwestern North America, just across the Bering Strait.

Though a few elk trickled over from Asia prior to the last glaciation, they couldn't compete with the vast numbers of much larger animals already grazing the plains. It wasn't until the ultimate predator, *Homo sapiens,* crossed the Bering Land Bridge and started killing off the true Pleistocene megafauna, that any deer grew abundant in North America.

Prior to the arrival of humans, and the long period of warmer weather that melted the ice (and still keeps it at bay), even New World deer like whitetails were relatively scarce, essentially specialists that lived in very limited habitat. But when North America changed, with both warmth and humans, the giant Pleistocene animals disappeared, and very quickly.

We have all heard that "nature abhors a vacuum." Into the vacuum of post-glacial North America poured new animals, including elk. They grew larger here, and along with other deer like caribou and mule deer, repopulated open country vacated by the disappearance of the Pleistocene megafauna.

Well, actually, one Pleistocene grazer survived, though in smaller form: the shrunken bison we know as the Plains buffalo. But after hundreds of thousands of years of domination by Rancholabrean giants, much of the New World opened up to deer, including the first of the "post-Pleistocene medium-fauna," the North American elk.

EVOLUTIONARY STRUCTURE

Further evidence of the elk's background comes from its build.

True plains animals, such as the American pronghorn and African oryx, have relatively short legs and run with their heads low. Since there's no need to jump over logs or rocks on the flat grasslands, long legs would waste the energy needed to run long distances. There's also no need to hold their heads high to see over obstacles, so both pronghorns and oryx are built low, for both initial speed and endurance, because out on the flats the only way to escape predators is to outdistance them.

Elk have long legs, and hold their heads very high when running. They evolved not on the flat plains, but in steeper country where they had to jump rocks or fallen trees when running from wolves.

You may also hear that elk are grazers, eating grass as opposed to the twig-browsing whitetail and mule deer. While elk evolved in more open country than did the red deer of Europe, the elk's diet requires both the carbohydrates of grass and the minerals of woody plants. (Whitetails and mule

Unlike true open-country prey mammals such as pronghorns and oryx, elk have long legs and hold their heads high, the better to escape through broken terrain.

*E*lk disappeared from most of North America at about the same rate European settlers arrived. Elk disappeared first from their extreme southern range in the mountains of central Mexico, where they may have held on as late as 1600. Next they disappeared from what is now the eastern United States. Evidently elk were never abundant in the East, except in a few isolated mountainous regions. Despite the effort it must have taken to pursue them, their large size and tough hides made them desirable to European-American hunters. In the 18th century, elk first disappeared from the southern coastal area, from Georgia to North Carolina. William Bartram, the noted naturalist, traveled through Georgia in the 1770s and wrote even then, that elk had disappeared except for a few in the northern mountains.

Farther north, from Virginia to Vermont in the United States, and in Quebec and Ontario, elk persisted into the 19th century. They survived longest in the rugged mountains of both Pennsylvania (until 1870) and West Virginia (until 1875).

Native elk held on a little longer in some central states, partly because they were more abundant in some areas, espe-

cially in Minnesota. The last native Minnesota elk was killed in 1896, though a small herd drifted down from Manitoba in 1932. One problem throughout most of the East and Midwest was that elk weren't nearly as shy as white-tailed deer. Herds often invaded towns during hard winters, where they were killed indiscriminately, often with knives.

In the southwest, elk hung on longest in Arizona, gradually disappearing due both to uncontrolled hunting and overgrazing by cattle in the early 1900s. By then, elk only existed in a few remnant populations in California (where a few Tule elk had been protected on a private preserve since 1872), Colorado, Idaho, Montana, Oregon, Wyoming and Washington, and in Canada in Alberta and British Columbia. By far the largest herds lived in and around Yellowstone National Park and in the Jackson Hole area of Wyoming.

The naturalist Ernest Thompson Seton, writing in 1927, put the pre-European population of elk at 10 million, though even he admitted that number was at best an educated guess. By 1900, those millions had dwindled to less than 100,000. Most Western states and provinces completely closed

elk hunting for decades at the beginning of the 20th century.

But elk, given protection and food, reproduce rapidly. Even before World War I, elk numbers in Yellowstone and Jackson Hole had grown enough to start transplants. And once new populations were started in the best elk areas of other states, some of these elk were transplanted.

The Black Hills of South Dakota received 25 Jackson Hole elk in 1914, and another

DESTRUCTION AND RECONSTRUCTION

50 from the northern Yellowstone herd in 1919. By 1927, the Black Hills herd had grown to the point where it provided 44 to repopulate West Texas's Guadalupe Mountains. Elk continued to be transplanted until the 1960s, when most of the available habitat once again had elk. Today, thanks to the support of conservation organizations like the Boone and Crockett Club, which supported most of the early refuges and transplants, hunters now take more than 100,000 elk each autumn, more than existed on the entire continent 100 years ago. And the herds still continue to grow.

deer, incidentally, also eat both grass and twigs.) The general rule of the herbivore diet is that the bigger the body, the tougher the food an animal can digest, because the extra size of its digestive system allows more time for woody fiber to break down. Elk rank toward the large end of the world's plant-eating animals, so they can digest some pretty tough food.

Elk can be very large. Our elk originated in Asia, crossing to North America on the Bering Land Bridge. While a few fossils from around 40,000 years ago have been found in Alberta, the bulk of prehistoric elk-remains date from about 11,000 years ago, the end of the last Ice Age, when the Bering Land Bridge connecting Asia and North America was last open. This is when animals and humans (known now as Native Americans) arrived from Siberia. Our elk are identical to the Siberian "maral," the largest of the red deer family, which evolved for very cold climates. Body size helps retain heat in subzero weather, and the largest bulls weigh more than half a ton.

The largest Rocky Mountain bull I could find record of was killed in my native state of Montana and weighed 1,010 pounds before field-dressing, but the Manitoba subspecies that inhabits the aspen country of the southern Canadian provinces may be the largest race, which makes sense because they live in the coldest climate. When weighed at the same time of year, a sample of mature Manitoba-race bulls from Elk Island National Park in eastern Alberta averaged 832 pounds, vs. 755 pounds for Rocky Mountain bulls from the Banff area of the province. The heaviest Elk Island bull weighed 1,034 pounds after losing almost all of its fat during the rut. Manitoba elk also have the largest skulls of any subspecies, a good indicator of average size.

But all North American elk are big animals. The Roosevelt elk of the northwest coastal mountains is often very large-bodied; the heaviest elk I could find a verified record of was a 1,110-pound Roosevelt from the transplanted herd on Alaska's Afognak Island. Even the "dwarf" Tule elk of California can weigh 700 pounds or more when living in lush country rather than the semi-desert of the central valley.

A mature bull elk can weigh 1,000 pounds, among the largest land animals of North America.

SPLITTERS VS. LUMPERS

Many modern biologists, using DNA analysis, have come to believe that all our elk subspecies are not really subspecies at all. Though North American elk vary slightly in appearance, they all live in different environments—from extremely cold prairie provinces to Wyoming mountainsides to the Pacific rainforest to the Sacramento Valley. Transplant Tule elk to Alberta, and in a few years they'd likely grow larger, perhaps as large as Alberta's native Rocky Mountain elk.

As the "lumpers" (those who believe all elk are one species) make inroads against the "splitters" in wildlife classification, our elk have lost their separate species designation of *Cervus canadensis*, given by a splitter named Borowski in 1780. Today North American elk are considered a

AN ELK BY ANY OTHER NAME

The word "elk" is derived from many Teutonic variations on the word that is applied in Europe to the animal we know as the moose, *Alces alces*. Moose inhabit much of northern Europe—especially Scandinavia, where it is known as the *alg*—but not the British Isles, which explains why the first English immigrants to New England called the first big deer they saw "elk." The red deer of the British Isles are among the smallest of their species, often no larger than the North American mule deer, so when the Pilgrims and other New Englanders saw 800-pound deer, they assumed they must be something like the legendary elk of Europe.

It's believed that the roots of the word elk come from the Greek *alce* (which, again confusingly, is the root of the moose's Linnaen name). *Alce*, in turn, became the old German *elaho*, eventually metamorphosing into *elg*, *elch* or *elen*. In Old English, the word became *eolh*, in Middle English, *alke*. In Old Irish, the word was *elit*, while in Czech, the red deer stag became *jelen*. And in America, all of these became *elk*.

But in early journals, other words were also used, and often translated into other languages. The Italian Verrazano referred to "stags, deer and hares" in New England, at least according to one English translation.

The forest-evolved Euro-Asian red deer is so closely related to elk that crossbreeds are fertile.

subspecies of the red deer: Many biologists consider the Rocky Mountain elk (*Cervus elaphus canadensis*), Manitoba elk (*C. e. manitobensis*), Roosevelt elk (*C. e. roosevelti*), Tule elk (*C. e. nannodes*) and the extinct Eastern (also *canadensis*) and Merriam's elk (*C. e. merriami*) of the Southwest all to be simple geographic races of the same animal rather than separate subspecies.

Does the "stag" refer to elk, which resemble the red stag? If so, then what are the deer—whitetails? Probably, but we'll never know. Sir Francis Drake wrote in 1579 that "infinite was the company of very large and fat Deere, which we saw by thousands ..." The word "thousands" implies herds, which would imply elk rather than whitetails, which tend toward smaller groups that remain more hidden than the meadow-loving elk.

Again, who knows? But by the mid-1600s many Europeans and European-Americans called this large stag "elk," though even then some new Americans liked to look down their nose at this common name. John Lederer, traveling through Virginia in 1670, saw "numerous herds of Red Deer (for their unusual largeness termed Elk by ignorant people) ..."

Despite such snobbery, by the early 1800s elk had become the common name; indeed, Lewis and Clark always called them that in their journals, expecting everybody to know what they meant. Still there were protests, even as the Corps of Discovery returned to St. Louis in 1806. In that year B.S. Barton, writing in the *Philadelphia Medical and Physical Journal*, suggested calling our elk "wapiti," a Shawnee word. Indeed, he went so far as to rearrange the Linnaen name for elk once again, to *Cervus wapiti*, which did not stick.

Indeed, the name wapiti, despite occasional use, is for all practical purposes almost as dead as "Virginia deer" for whitetail. In the Wildlife Management Institute's fine book, *Elk of North America*, Larry Bryant and Chris Maser say that the term "wapiti is mainly used by the authors of papers that have international significance and by romantic magazine writers." Since I doubt this "paper" has any international significance, I'll use elk.

But I must recall my friend Chet Wheelless's suggestion, when we were both wildlife biology students at the University of Montana and I was a struggling freelance writer, that I write a children's book entitled *Hippity-Hoppity, Let's Hunt a Wapiti*. Which is still the best use I've ever seen of the Shawnee name.

SOCIAL STRUCTURE OF AN ELK HERD

*I*n addition to being very large and highly adaptable, North American elk have a number of social characteristics that are interesting to biologists and vital to any hunter searching for antlers and meat.

Elk live in large herds, called "selfish herds" by biologists. Prey animals in large selfish herds don't band together to protect each other. Rather, those herds tend to protect individuals because any one animal is less likely to be singled out by a predator: There is, relatively speaking, some safety in numbers because one of your herd mates is more likely to get singled out.

"Selfish herd" theory says that large-herd deer, especially those living in relatively open country, will grow large antlers, designed by evolution more as advertisements to female deer than as weapons. Humans may see huge antlers as threatening (not to mention desirable), but in the day-to-day life of herbivores around the world, the larger the antlers or horns, the worse they work as weapons.

Remember the ancestral tusked deer? The antlerless tusked deer of today—such as the water deer of China and Korea—do far more damage to other water deer than bull elk do to each other, or any predator. In fact, elk tend to kick at predators rather than use their antlers.

While bull elk have been known to wound and even kill each other, their fights tend to be far rarer and less bloody than those of the much smaller white-tailed deer. Whitetails live in thick cover, so bucks don't need huge antlers to advertise their worth to distant does. Instead, whitetail antlers are used more for serious fighting between males during the autumn rut. Mule deer live in more open country, so they have larger antlers than whitetails, and also fight less.

The enormous antlers of bull elk say to any available cow: "Here's a

The large antlers of elk serve more as social calling cards than weaponry: proof of a herd bull's fitness to sire calves. Cow elk tend to choose large-antlered bulls during the autumn rut.

really capable fellow who not only knows good food but defends it from other bulls." And bull elk actually need richer food than cows. Why? Because to grow their huge bone-advertisements during the brief northern summer, they need enormous amounts of calcium and phosphate. And their larger bodies need to grow muscle and fat to survive the September rut. After the rut, bulls tend to live in small groups in isolated areas, where small meadows provide the wide variety of high-quality food they require. Cows live near larger meadows, where their large "selfish" herds protect them from predation and where they can eat lots of lower-quality food to feed their growing fetuses.

Antlers are bone, and the long, dense antlers of bull elk must grow over a short period each summer.

MOBILITY: ELK RHYTHMS

All these evolutionary characteristics affect where and why elk live in certain areas throughout the year. Their nutritional and mating rhythms profoundly affect where they can be found during autumn. Twenty years ago I had a girlfriend who worked for the U.S. Forest Service as an archaeologist, so she spent much of her summers in the mountains looking for old log cabins and Indian artifacts. On these trips she often saw herds of elk.

During late-summer backyard parties when a bunch of men (including me) gathered around the barbecue or the beer keg and started discussing just when and where we would hunt elk in September or October or November, she would speak right up and say she knew where a whole pile of elk lived, so what was the big deal? She'd tell us exactly where to find 'em.

What she never understood was that since elk are big and live in herds, they can eat themselves out of a particular kind of food in short order. Because elk have long legs and great strength they can travel several mountains on a whim—or on a search for another kind of food. And elk are large: When they shed their thin, coppery summer coats in late August and grow thick, hollow hair in preparation for the subzero cold and deep snow of November, they don't like living in warm summer meadows anymore.

I later married Eileen, a woman who likes to eat elk meat. We still live in elk country, and over the years of both marriage and hunting we've found where "our" elk live during warm spring days, with their new calves by their sides. We know when the bulls' antlers will branch, because using a 40X spotting scope we often see several summer-red bull elk bedded together on a high ridge, their blunt-tipped, blood-gorged antlers covered with a fine fur much like that covering their fat ribs. In the fall, we know where those same bulls use their antlers to rip apart young and innocent pine trees, or bed on days when arctic air drifts down from Canada.

We know the rhythms of elk, because knowing those rhythms feeds us. The grass the elk eat in June feeds us in December, and so another year turns.

If you'd like to come along and follow the elk year, feel welcome. ✳

Mature bulls, whose growing antlers are tender and easily damaged, will stick to less-dense stands of timber when they take cover during summer. Here a bull licks sap from a small tree that was horned the previous fall.

Part One

THE RUT

SOUND *of the* WILD

It was the commencement of the rutting season with the Elk when the Bucks frequently utter a loud cry resembling a shrill whistle especially when they see anything of a strange appearance. We had made our beds at night on a little bench between two small dry gullies. The weather was clear and the moon shone brightly about 10 at night when I supposed my comrades fast asleep an Elk blew his shrill whistle within about 100 yards of us. I took my gun slipped silently into the gully and crept towards the place where I heard the sound but I soon found he had been frightened by the horses and ran off up the Mountain. On turning back I met Allen who hearing the Elk had started to get a shot at him in the same manner I had done without speaking a word. We went back to Camp but our Camp keeper was no where to be found. We searched the bushes high and low ever and anon calling for "Conn" but no "Conn" answered. At length Allen cruising thro the brush tumbled over a pile of rubbish when lo! Conn was beneath nearly frightened out of his wits. "Arrah! an it is you Allen" Said he trembling as if an ague fit was shaking him "but I thought the whole world was full of the spalpeens of savages And where are they gone?"

—Osborne Russell,
Journal of a Trapper,
September 15, 1837

The "bugle" of a bull elk doesn't sound anything like a bugle. It may not even include a whistle, especially late in the rut, when a hoarse herd bull might merely bray like a donkey.

There are a few wild sounds emitted by wild animals that instantly touch even the most urban among us.

Today, at the beginning of the 21st century, many of us can hear the gobble of wild turkeys or the yips of coyotes on the edges of cities. If we travel far enough into the wilderness of this still half-wild planet, we can hear wolves howl and lions roar. Both reach somewhere deep inside us, to the particles of ancient human DNA that yearn to throw another branch on the fire, to push back the darkness.

I have heard all these sounds, and each still snaps my head to attention. But some people simply do not recognize them, mistaking coyotes for dogs, or lions for thunder, their ignorant hearts pumping calmly even amid the sounds of the wild.

But to paraphrase Aldo Leopold, I would not want to know the human whose heart does not beat hard at the breeding call of a bull elk. It is a sound unmistakable for any other, a sound that always thrills—or even frightens—as it did poor "Conn," who thought it the cries of young

The whistle portion of a bull elk's mating call carries farther in open country than the low grunts preceding it. The deep grunts communicate with nearby elk, especially a bull's own harem.

Native Americans.

The mating call of a bull elk is usually called a bugle, though it resembles no bugle you have ever heard, and it isn't restricted to the "shrill whistle" described by Osborne Russell. I have heard September bull elk that sounded like a donkey braying into an oil drum, or like a bull buffalo roaring, or even like a rubber band snapped against an empty coffee can. But the elk's shrill whistle is the sound that brings our heads up and makes our hearts beat harder.

ANATOMY ∮ A BUGLE

To make the sound, a bull leans his head back, opens his mouth wide to expose teeth and tongue, and forces air from his throat across his lower incisors. The resulting whistle can carry for miles on a still morning.

A young spike or "raghorn" bull may only whistle, but a mature bull begins his bugle with a rasping roar that begins in his lungs, and often ends the whistle with a series of belly-deep grunts. A rough phonetic version of a classic big bull's bugle is something like "rrrrrRRREEEEeee, eeYUH, eeYUH, eeYUH." The rougher, deeper parts of the sound resonate at closer ranges, communicating with nearby elk, while the whistle contacts distant elk.

(The European red deer, which evolved in forests, rather than in the mixture of timber and open grassland that formed the Siberian and North American elk, doesn't whistle but "roars," covering its lower teeth with its lips while opening its mouth, forming a nearly closed resonating chamber. Nearby, this does indeed sound like a roar, and resembles the bull-bellowing that big elk often emit toward the end of the rut when their whistling-machinery may be hoarse. But at a few hundred yards the red deer's roar sounds more like a prolonged and exaggerated belch, the sort that some

An elk bugles with his mouth wide open, allowing air to whistle over his lower incisors.

7th-grade boys love to mimic—and it doesn't carry much farther.)

Many stories tell of a bugling bull elk sending his "challenge" to other bulls on the same mountain. This sounds rough and romantic, but most bull elk are hardly spoiling for a fight, like some drunk in a bar. So why do they bugle? From all the evidence, elk fill the September air with whistles for the same reasons birds sing in spring: to attract females, to warn off other males, and to make themselves feel better in general.

BULLS CALL, COWS CHOOSE

As with most organisms more complex than amoebas, female elk actually choose their male mates. Subtle and not-so-subtle signs of male health allow females to pick only bulls that seem healthy—bulls that have eaten well and will likely produce strong, healthy offspring. Two immediately apparent signs of good health in bull elk are tall, evenly-matched antlers and a loud bugle.

But while the females do the ultimate choosing, the rutting sequence in many large temperate-zone mammals actually begins with changes in the males. The elk rut truly begins in mid-August, when the male elk's testosterone level rises, spurred by shorter days. For three months or more the bulls have been growing their antlers, and hanging out together peacefully, thanks to higher levels of the "female" hormone estrogen. But as summer wanes, their rising level of "male" testosterone shuts down the flow of blood to their antlers. The fine-haired skin we call "velvet" dies, and peels from the now-hard bone underneath.

The suddenly hard-antlered bulls abruptly find the other bulls they spent the summer with kind of obnoxious. Their antlers hard and insensitive, they start sparring with each other in tests of strength and bugling.

At least part of the function of bugling is to attract cows. I suspect that cow-attraction bugles receive less attention than they should, probably because they're not often witnessed. But I've seen a bull call in a willing cow more than once, especially in Yellowstone Park, the world's finest

A bull elk calls for several reasons, but mostly to attract females. Instead of commanding their presence, he's actually requesting their attention. If his antlers match his silver tongue, cows will join his harem.

laboratory for semi-wild elk watching. The first time, the sequence was quite plain. A big herd bull, unusual because he only had five long tines on each antler rather than the more standard six, was tending a dozen cows and calves along the meadowed banks of the Madison River. It was mid-September, when mature bulls first start gathering cows, and no younger bulls had found this bunch yet. The big five-point had them all to himself, so there was no apparent reason for him to bugle every two or three minutes. But he did, and Eileen and I sat and watched from across the river, occasionally taking a photograph when he tilted his head back and screamed.

After half an hour of this, the bull bugled again. But then his body language changed. Until then he'd been almost lazy, perfunctorily calling once in a while just to keep in practice. But now, after his last bugle, his body stiffened, and he leaned his head for-ward, looking up the valley like an 800-pound bird dog.

We followed his eyes upstream, but couldn't see anything. Almost imme-diately, the bull bugled again, insis-tently. Then I heard the faint sound of cow-talk, much like the "meow" of a curious cat. The bull looked hard toward the sound for a moment, then lifted his head and bugled again, and a lone cow walked out of the timber, 200 yards up the meadow. The bull bugled quickly, then trotted toward her a few yards. The rest of his herd munched lazily on the long meadow grass, ignoring the whole display. But over the next minute the bull very definitely "bugled in" the lone cow. She kept calling back as she walked nearer, mewing every few seconds until she joined the harem. Only then did a couple of the bull's previ-ous cows lift their heads and cau-tiously approach the newcomer, sniff-ing her lightly, then accepting her into the herd.

A bull elk's harem can include from one cow to more than two dozen elk, though not all will be cows of breeding age. It may even include an occasional pre-adolescent bull. Here a bull watches over his harem on the banks of the Athabasca River, Alberta.

THREE STAGES OF THE RUT

That moment was the tail end of what might be termed the elk "pre-rut," to borrow a phrase from serious hunters of white-tailed deer. As with whitetails, the elk rut breaks down into three definite phases: pre-rut, breeding rut and post-rut.

Pre-rut begins with the peeling antlers and first bugles of late August. Here, nature is priming the males. Unlike human men and some other male primates, bull elk (and buck deer and hundreds of other mammals) are normally physically incapable of breeding all year round.

Once bulls lose their velvet, however, they also become fertile. By the middle of September, when the first few cows normally come into estrus, the bulls are ready and willing. Over the next month, almost every cow will have bred with these males; 80 percent of the cows will be impregnated within a two-week period. This ensures that most of the calves will be born the next spring, just when the first tender shoots are erupting from the lower valleys' winter-dormant pastures. The cows will have enough fresh green food to produce rich milk, and so many calves will be on the ground that predators won't be able to eat the whole crop, which could easily happen if the calves were born over a three-month period.

All of these factors increase the odds that enough calves will survive each year and eventually reproduce—the ultimate measure of success in nature. But the system means the bulls have to be ready when the first cows come into heat. Otherwise they can't pass down their genetic code, and will have failed as bull elk.

Bull elk become ready to breed as their antlers harden, due to a change in hormone levels. They also begin to act aggressively, often attacking young conifers, which removes loose velvet from antlers and strengthens neck muscles for the pushing matches of the upcoming rut.

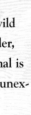

Bull elk enter September at their heaviest weight of the year, sometimes weighing as much as 1,000 pounds. Over the summer they've stuffed themselves with

A Quick, Sure-Fire Weight Loss Program

high-carbohydrate green grasses, sometimes putting on more than 200 pounds of fat. Sleek, plump and lazy all at the same time, they soon start a quick weight-loss program combining exercise and less eating.

The biggest bulls in a herd quite simply eat almost nothing from the time their harems are gathered in mid- to late-September until almost all the cows are bred in mid-October. While passing up meals, they're also running a lot, herding cows

back into their harem and chasing away other bulls. Combine heavy exercise with fewer calories, and the fat bulls of early September can look gaunt, disheveled and even wounded a month later.

Not only do the bulls lose almost all their fat, but they've also been wallowing in mud baths, urinating on themselves and fighting other bulls. Their ribs stick out, they stink and their hair's uncombed. Their chests and necks are full of scars, scabs and pus-filled wounds, and sometimes their antlers are chipped and broken. In short, they're a mess.

They also aren't particularly tasty at this time. Grizzly bears, mountain lions and wolves often take down exhausted bulls now, but the human hunters who tag a herd bull any time in October through early November usually find the meat tough and somewhat musky tasting. Consequently, some people think all big elk taste this way, when the musky flavor is actually a seasonal aberration caused by dramatic weight loss. Any animal, wild or domestic, has more tender, tastier meat when the animal is gaining weight and adding unex-

ercised muscle to its frame.

If you're interested in fine meat—and elk is some of the finest, wild or tame—don't kill a mature bull during that month and a half. But killed anytime in September, big elk still tend to taste fine, and by mid-November they've been eating again for a month, putting on as much muscle and fat as they can before winter. Or take a cow or younger bull. Many bowhunters will try for a big bull until the harems form in late September, then they'll switch to a search for a cow, spike or 2½-year-old "raghorn" bull; these animals don't usually rut hard, and usually keep gaining weight all fall.

THE ACTUAL PEAK OF THE RUT

Hunters have long been attracted to bugling bull elk, especially the big herd bulls. A deep, throaty bugle not only tells us where a bull is, but indicates (without guaranteeing) a mature body and, hence, large antlers. Ever since "sport" hunters began pursuing bull elk, the prime time to hunt big-antlered bulls has been considered the peak of the bugling season.

But by the time the mountains echo with elk music, most bigger bulls have already gathered their harems of cows. In most years, the actual peak of bugling coincides with the period when most cows first come into estrus, typically late September. The peak of the actual breeding rut, when most cows become pregnant, can be deduced by observing when most calves are born in spring, then subtracting the approximately 250- to 260-day gestation period. In my home state of Montana, a typical Rocky Mountain elk state, biologists have found that about 80 percent of breeding occurs between September 25th and October 10th, slightly later than the last-half-of-September period most hunters generally consider the peak bugling season.

There's an excellent reason for this. Most bugling occurs while the bulls are gathering harems and first defending them from other bulls. After the harems have formed, herd bulls don't have to bugle as much to attract cows, and after the actual rut starts they don't have as much time to mouth off, since they're spending more time actually courting and breeding estrous cows.

During the peak of the rut, mature bull elk often lose 20% of their body weight, due both to exercise (chasing cows and other bulls) and lack of eating.

THE BEST TIME
TO CALL IN BULLS

What does all of this mean to the hunter? Several things. Most important is the fact that the pre-rut is probably the best time to call in a bull—and especially a mature "herd" bull—rather than at the peak of the rut.

Why is this? During the rut's peak, herd bulls will be surrounded not only by their harem of cows and calves (and, as we shall see, the odd immature bull), but younger "satellite" bulls who hang out within a few hundred yards of the big bull's harem, waiting to cut out a few cows for themselves. These other elk are all centered around the herd bull, like the planets around the sun. Combine all those noses with the vagaries of mountain breezes, and it

becomes awfully difficult to approach herd bulls, especially close enough for a shot with a bow. And except for a few wilderness areas, most center-fire rifle or even muzzleloader seasons these days take place past the peak of the rut. Unless blessed with enough wealth to afford a rut-hunt on private land in New Mexico, most of us will be hunting rutting elk with stick and string.

So among serious bowhunters, the consensus is that the best time to get close to a bull elk is during the pre-rut, when bulls are actively seeking cows. Not only are the bulls alone instead of being surrounded by a dozen or more other elk, but they respond more easily to a cow call.

This type of elk call, the "meow" previously mentioned, revolutionized rut-hunting of elk. I first started cow-calling almost twenty years ago, using a mouth-diaphragm (the type used to call turkeys) until I could reproduce not only a bull's bugle, but the questioning meow of a cow searching for a bull. I called in elk my first two seasons but never got quite the right shot, mostly because I was a very particular bowhunter.

But on the evening of September 5th, opening day of my third season, during the early part of the pre-rut, I found a lone five-point bull feeding in a meadow on a long ponderosa ridge in central Montana. He was out there maybe 250 yards, with a slight breeze coming from him to me, so I cupped my hands around my mouth and cow-called as loudly as I could. He picked up his head and looked my way. I called again, more insistently, and he started walking toward me. Kneeling behind a small pine on the edge of the timber, I watched the bull through the screen of thin branches.

Whenever he halted or hesitated, I called again. After about five minutes he finally eased up within 40 yards, standing almost broadside, looking for the cow he knew must be in the timber. The sun had just set behind him and I couldn't see the sight-pins of

Bull elk come most readily to either a bugle or cow call before they have actually gathered harems. A cow call can also be amplified by a grunt tube, attracting bulls up to half a mile away.

In the past 20 years, as elk numbers have increased across the West and more hunters travel from other parts of the country to hunt them, many hunting articles

WHITETAIL TACTICS?

have told new elk hunters that "whitetail tactics" can help them take elk. This is heartening to a whitetail hunter from east of the Mississippi, who can be intimidated by both elk country and the new ways of this huge deer they're hunting.

There is some truth to the suggestion. More than most other western big game animals, elk tend to bed in thick cover for protection from both weather and predators. So hunters who've grown up learning to sneak very slowly through timber—the classic still-hunting tactic of the whitetail hunter, especially in the Northeast—often find some success.

But two factors make this advice highly debatable. While out tromping around the local mountains, I've run into eastern elk hunters who, after several days of carefully still-hunting "black" timber, have been not only skunked, but haven't even

seen one of those dad-blasted wapiti. There is a simple reason for this: There aren't any elk where they're still-hunting.

Elk have much larger territories than do white-tailed deer. One particular herd will gladly travel three canyons over in order to avoid hunters. A spooked whitetail will often just run a few hundred yards and bed down again, but spooked elk can travel several miles over a 3,000-foot ridge before settling down. There are exceptions (which we'll get to in a moment), but slowly still-hunting a mountain over three or four days can easily result in no elk sightings, because that mountain is totally elkless.

The other problem with the "whitetail tactics" advice is that too many of today's whitetail hunters don't have a clue how to still-hunt, since they've grown up hiding in treestands, waiting for one of the superabundant deer to walk by. While you can stand-hunt for elk, you really need local knowledge to do it, mostly of the escape routes elk use when traveling from one mountain to another while avoiding hunters, though bowhunters can often effectively stand-hunt in dry country during the heat of early fall, especially near waterholes. Elk do need lots of water, particularly during the rut.

One old-time elk hunter claimed that a herd of spooked

elk won't stop until it crosses running water. There's probably some truth to that, both because crossing a stream can divert scent-trailing predators like wolves, and because elk get thirsty while running.

But some hunters of big bull elk have claimed that mature bulls are the easiest to find after being jumped. Why? In the first couple of weeks after the rut, when many rifle seasons open, herd bulls are still relatively weak from the rigors of chasing and mating and fighting. They don't want to run over the top of a mountain. Instead, they'll often trot off a quarter mile or so, then stop and watch their backtrail, just like a big whitetail buck. The trick then is not to follow their backtrail, but circle toward where you think the elk may be, approaching from the side. Quite often, a bull will stop in the first cover on the far side of a clearing, and turn to watch the clearing. If you can successfully still-hunt through the timber around the far side of the clearing's edge, you may catch the bull standing broadside, watching where you aren't.

my bow against his black silhouette, so I aimed above his long back, then lowered the 40-yard pin behind his shoulder and released. After a heartbeat there came a sound like canvas tearing, and the bull whirled and trotted across the meadow, head held high like a camel. After 100 yards he slowed, then started stumbling sideways and finally fell, rolling completely over, his long legs turning skyward in a cloud of fine dust. When I tried to stand, my own knees did not really want to do their job.

Elk can be hunted with whitetail tactics—if there are elk in the neighborhood. Every ridge in deer country tends to hold deer. The same cannot be said of elk range.

HEAT ❧ SEPTEMBER ELK

While very early September can be a good time to kill any bull, it's still a little early for the big herd bulls to be interested. They can be coaxed in, but they tend to live in very specific places at this time of year, especially on public land where they've learned through years of experience that September means the hills will be full of humans dressed like trees.

In most ways, September is hard on big bull elk. They're being chased by bowhunters, many of whom have no clue about what they're doing and who also let their stink waft into every canyon, spooking bulls who not only have just grown their winter coat but are as fat as the average sumo wrestler. A big bull in early September actually waddles when he runs, fat jiggling over his ribs like gelatin. He'll need that fat to get through the rut, because he won't get much chance to eat while bugling, courting cows and chasing away rival bulls.

So the big bulls are essentially insu-lated by fat and hair at a time of year when daytime temperatures often reach 70°F or higher, even in the high mountains. This evidently feels much like wearing a down coat while sitting next to a nice warm wood stove. So elk look for cool places, the tiny pieces of tall mountains and deep canyons that stay cool even dur-ing midday.

How cool does the air have to be? One Oregon study found that elk, any time after they acquired their winter coats, preferred temperatures of 55°F or lower. These cool places are not common in early September, even in the northern Rockies, but they do exist.

They exist mostly on the shaded north slopes of mountains. Early in September the sun still rises high at noon, but the backsides of steep mountains remain shaded. The shade is created both by ridgetops and the tall timber that normally grows on north slopes. Snow doesn't melt and rain doesn't evaporate as quickly on north slopes, so trees have more

---

Because of their big bodies and new winter coat, September elk seek cool shade, often around water. Spring hollows on the north slopes of mountain ridges are particularly favored.

water with which to grow. And because more snow and rain eases into the pine-needle duff, rather than evaporating as it does off barren south-slope meadows, little springs of cool groundwater flow from the side-canyons all along the north sides of mountain ridges.

The temperature of groundwater springs reflects the average year-round temperature of that area. In my part of Montana, most springs ease from the ground at 52°F, a few degrees lower than the comfort level of winter-haired elk. These little springs cool the surrounding air quite

effectively, especially if they well up under a canopy of pines or aspens, doubly so if they rise in a fairly level part of a little side-canyon. Trees and level ground both tend to pool the water-cooled atmosphere, like a naturally air-conditioned room.

It's astonishing how much cooler one of these dark, north-slope pockets can be than even the timber a few feet away on the surrounding side-ridges.

I've often dropped into one of these pockets, thirsty as hell after a hot day of hiking elkless ridges, and have been almost as grateful to find an empty pocket as I would if it were full of elk; without the need to sneak up on wapiti, I can just take a drink. Any of these little springs, filtered through hundreds of feet of mountain, is free of the invasive little beasties like giardia that make humans sick, so I always carry a water bottle that can be tilted into the small current. After sitting there a few minutes, listening to the quiet water-music and occasional chatter of a squirrel, I often start shivering as my sweaty body chills down. That's how cool these micro-pockets can be.

And that's why elk like them.

You can find these pockets easily, sometimes by just looking over a topographic map, sometimes by hiking and sometimes by simply walking the ridges and bugling down the north slopes until a bull answers. Unfortunately, mature bulls often pick spring-holes that simply cannot be reached any other way than by hiking straight down a very steep, thickly timbered mountain for a mile or two. If you're in good enough shape to be elk hunting, this isn't really a big problem. The problem comes when you get lucky enough to kill a big bull down there and have to pack 500 or more pounds of meat straight up the same mountain.

A few years ago, I bowhunted elk in the steep country of the Idaho panhandle with my friend Sandy Podsaid, who at the time was working with an outfitter in the area. We horse-packed into a high basin and camped in comfortable wall tents by a good-sized creek. There were plenty of elk around. We rode in on August 31st, the day before the season opened, and a herd of cows, calves

---

Because elk country is so large, and elk are herd animals, many hunters find maps and long-range optics useful. Both can save a lot of walking through elkless country.

and spikes came to drink from the creek that evening, right there in camp. But we never even saw a big bull all week, though we heard a few, bugling desultorily far down the steepest mountain above the Clearwater River, where Sandy said he would never take a packhorse unless he really wanted to kill it.

Far better is the second week of September, when most bulls start actively searching for cows, moving out of their micro-havens to the more open country where cows have been raising their calves all summer. Cow-calling is still the best way to attract one of these bulls, but in order to find one, a loud bugle still helps.

SPEAKING ELK

Bugling used to be the only way most hunters tried to attract bulls, using various calls to imitate the whistle and, eventually, the bugle-grunt sequence of bull elk. This worked—some of the time. After all, why would a bull looking for love search for another bull? The only logical reason would be to steal some cows.

But when the called bull came in, expecting to find somebody else's harem, he didn't see anything but trees, because the hunter was hunkered down behind a little ponderosa pine, hiding. So the bull "hung up,"

just out of range of arrow-shot. Or he didn't bother coming in at all, because he already had some cows.

Despite all this, and despite often primitive calling equipment, hunters bugled in and killed many bull elk each year. Actually, some of the hunting bugles used in the "old days" weren't as bad as hip, modern elk hunters would have us believe.

The most popular commercial elk bugle was a piece of small-diameter pipe, often a piece of copper or plastic conduit, bent into a circle. The hunter blew into one end, the air passing over the ribs of the conduit

Thirty years ago hunters almost exclusively imitated the whistle of a bull elk. While a bull's whistle is still effective today, more hunters use the wide variety of elk sounds made not only by bulls, but by cows and calves as well.

and producing a thin whistle that rose or dropped in pitch, depending on how hard the hunter blew. These "pigtail" calls are often mocked by modern hunters who prefer using diaphragm mouth calls or commercial cow calls, but the pigtail calls sounded very much like the thin whistle of a young bull.

One scientifically minded experimenter found, through sonogram analysis of a pigtail call, that the various pitches of its whistles actually mimicked the whistle of an elk better than the highly touted mouth diaphragm. Elk, like many mammals, can hear tones the human ear can't, and the pigtail reproduced these tones more closely than any other commercial call.

But during the peak of the bugling years, hunters found that a mouth diaphragm could reproduce any sound an elk makes, including the hoarse whistle and deep grunt of a big bull. Soon thousands of hunters were blowing through long "grunt tubes" about 2 inches in diameter, in order to amplify the bugle-grunt and make it sound as resonant as the deep-chested call of a big bull. "Elk-calling" contests became all the rage, with contestants trying to out-scream and out-grunt each other. I suppose this is natural. After all, what male elk hunter doesn't, at some level, identify with a big herd bull?

But over the next few years many hunters came to the conclusion that the thin, gruntless whistles of young bulls often worked better in attracting other bulls. Why? Because a deep-

Commercial elk calls can imitate almost any elk vocalization, especially the sounds bulls and cows make during the rut.

throated bugle, followed by a series of harsh grunts, signified a big bull to other elk. As mentioned earlier, bugling bull elk are not "challenging" other bulls—at least not most of the time. Instead, they're advertising for cows. When a herd bull hears another big bull bugle nearby, his natural

reaction is to gather up his cows and leave. Bull elk normally receive several dozen antler-wounds during the rut, but not because they want to. The high, pure call of a young bull, on the other hand, often convinces another bull that here's a young fellow who can be easily divested of his cows.

Once the harems are gathered in late September, bugling and cow-calling bring in far more "satellite" bulls than herd bulls. Satellites are the younger bulls that hang around the edges of harems, hoping to snag a wandering cow. Sometimes they even hang out inside the harem. Spike elk—those

$1\frac{1}{2}$-year-old bulls with their first set of antlers—accompany their mothers until the rut, when they're normally run off by bigger bulls.

But spikes are equivalent to young boys just entering puberty. While some "advanced" spikes become fertile their first antlered fall, many don't; others are somewhere in between, with low sperm counts. You'll see this reflected in their antlers. Some spikes have hard antlers, just like mature bulls, while others retain all or most of their velvet until their spikes are shed that winter.

The effort of gathering a harem is nothing compared to the energy required in keeping and defending it. A bull sometimes succeeds in gathering a very large harem at the beginning of the rut, only to have some cows "stolen" as he tires over the next few weeks.

When diminished elk populations truly recovered, during and after World War II, most general seasons allowed hunters to take any bull, including spikes. But as hunting pressure increased in the 1970s, game managers found that elk numbers in some areas were shrinking despite low cow harvests. At first the biologists suspected poaching or disease, but researchers eventually found that in many areas, bulls were being killed as soon as they grew antlers. While there were theoretically enough bulls to impregnate the cows—one bull will easily breed with 10 or 15 females each season—calf production was way down in some areas. Research showed that in those regions, most of the breeding was done by spike bulls, and spikes often aren't fully fertile.

The solution has varied from state to state, and even in areas of the same state.

The Montana valley where I live is bisected by the upper Missouri River. The hunting area on the east side of the river allows only the taking of "brow-tined" bulls, with a tine at 4 inches long on the bottom half of one antler. This normally indicates a $2\frac{1}{2}$-year-old bull. These bulls are quite fertile, and since they weren't killed as spikes the previous fall, they have survived to breed with cows this September and October. While a few are taken during bow

FERTILITY AND ELK MANAGEMENT

season, most do survive until the November rifle season, when almost all are taken each year. But by the next fall, another crop of spikes has grown into breeding bulls.

On the west side of the valley, only spikes are legal during the general season, with a few dozen "any elk" permits allowed by drawing each year. The result is that spikes who survive their first hunting season often reach full maturity. That hunting area contains a lot of mature 6-point bulls, which do most of the breeding. Both solutions offer a general season where any resident with an elk tag can kill a meat bull, but the spike-only side of the valley also allows a rare lottery chance at a big herd bull.

Much is made of fights between big bull elk during the rut, but antlerless elk fight too. It isn't uncommon to see cows and calves lash out at each other with their front hooves, or even stand on their hind legs, ears laid back and teeth

FIGHTING ISN'T JUST BETWEEN BULLS

gnashing, to "box" each other. This happens most often when elk crowd together around some prime food or mineral lick, and occasionally when bedding down in steep country, where comfortable flat beds are hard to find.

Most often older, higher-ranking cows simply shove aside lesser-ranking animals, especially calves. Sometimes cows also fight when they feel cornered, as when a rutting herd bull tries to push them together in a certain direction. Cows also turn very aggressive when they are about to give birth and want to run off last year's calf.

"Domestic" elk can be very aggressive toward humans. I've known two elk ranchers. One said that except during the rut, he worried more about the cows than the bulls. When working inside his elk corrals, he always watched for signs of aggression, such as laid-back ears and gnashing teeth. But he said that often a cow would lash out with a front hoof without warning. A hoof-slash from a big cow can break arms or even flay open flesh and major arteries.

Another rancher turned his back once on a big bull during the rut. The bull charged and knocked him down, then tried to gore the rancher with his antlers. Luckily, the edge of the corral interfered with the bull's thrusts, and the man was actually able to grab the antlers and hold the bull off him while he lay on the ground and shouted for help. He was lucky to get away with minor scrapes and

bruises. A big bull can kill another bull, and on open ground, a truly aggressive bull wouldn't find a human much of a problem.

Bulls also can direct their anger toward any other threat, especially during the rut. On an August family visit to Yellowstone Park in my teens, we found a big bull feeding by himself in a meadow along the Madison River, 100 yards from the highway, and my father started taking 8mm home movies. About that time, a man pulled up in a station wagon, calmly collected his little Kodak camera, snapped a leash on a full-grown redbone hound, then took his dog out into the meadow after the elk.

The elk looked up as the man and dog approached within about 30 feet. Until then, the hound had been lifting his leg on various clumps of grass, but when the bull raised its head the dog rushed forward, barking, and the man could barely hold him on the leash. The bull didn't run; instead it lowered its head like a Spanish fighting bull and thumped a front hoof on the ground. Luckily the man took the hint and dragged his dog away, but if he'd tried the same stunt a month later the bull might not have been so patient. Every autumn in Yellowstone, people are charged and sometimes sent up trees by rutting bulls.

HAREMS ARE NOT ALWAYS GIRLS-ONLY

One fall I bowhunted a herd in the Little Belt Mountains of west-central Montana. A really big herd bull, with six tines on one antler and seven on the other, had gathered a harem of 29 smaller elk, including 18 cows, 11 calves and one spike, still in the velvet. I found them one evening while glassing from a rocky knob on one side of a high canyon. Just after sunset I found one cow grazing in a grassy saddle across the canyon, just below a finger of mature Douglas fir timber. After a couple of minutes, a few more cows and calves trotted out of the timber, followed by the herd bull, poking the rump of the last cow with his long antlers.

As soon as that last cow trotted into the meadow, the big bull turned and trotted back into the trees. That's when a spike, unnoticed in the midst of all those cows and calves, hopped up on the back of one of the cows and tried to breed her.

He wasn't up there long. In a few seconds another batch of cows came running out of the timber, the herd bull behind them. As soon as the spike saw the big bull, he jumped off the cow and stood staring casually across the canyon, as if he hadn't begun to think of girls. The big bull turned back into the timber again, and the spike jumped back up on "his" cow.

But the herd-master was evidently watching from inside the trees, and he came out grunting like a Hereford bull. The little spike left the cow and ran downhill 75 yards. The herd bull was evidently satisfied with that distance, and started wandering among his 28 cows and calves, licking the rump of one cow in particular, who must have been just about to come into heat. This was on October 1st, the very peak of the breeding season.

I hunted that herd for three afternoons, and they came out of the same patch of timber every evening. No, I never did get the big bull, and actually at that point of the season was more interested in one of his cows. But I never did see the spike try to mount one of the females again.

It's a fact of bull elk life: Autumn is for watching over and protecting your harem, breeding with each cow as she comes into heat, and running off any other bulls—big or small—who want in on the action.

THE MATING DANCE

Bulls continue their rump-lick courting behavior for hours and sometimes even a full day before a cow is ready to breed. But once she's ready there's not much ceremony.

I once watched a huge 7x7 bull breed a cow on the National Bison Range near Moiese, Montana. (The Bison Range was established for the preservation of buffalo early in the century, but also has fine herds of elk, deer, pronghorn and bighorn sheep, along with a few black bears and mountain goats.) Evidently, I started watching just as the courtship ended, for suddenly the bull jumped up on the back of the cow, wrapping his front legs around her ribs, then thrust himself at her rump so violently that all four rear elk hooves—his and hers—left the ground. Then he

The mating of elk is quick and almost violent; the cow's hind legs are often lifted right off the ground. An observer will miss the whole show in only a few seconds of inattention.

While elk antlers are large and imposing, they function mostly to impress cows, not to fight other bulls. Most of the pecking order is worked out during the pre-rut, in light sparring "fights" or simple posturing by the larger bulls. But fights do happen, especially in populations where the mature bull ratio is high, such as in Yellowstone Park. There are enough bulls per cow in the park that serious arguments over an estrous female occur frequently, and the fights tend to be more serious and occasionally even fatal. Almost all Yellowstone bulls taken during late Montana and Wyoming hunting seasons, when they leave the deep snows of the park, show dozens of antler scars.

But in average populations, where the ratio of big bulls to cows is fairly low, rut-fights are rare. Fewer bulls are seriously wounded, and the animals are generally in better condition to survive the winter. Consequently, while the number of mature bulls in the Yellowstone population is often higher than in many National Forests, the overall percentage of bulls in the population may be almost the same. Many Yellowstone bulls die of wounds, malnourishment or predation over the winter because the stress of the rut is much more severe. Rarely does any elk herd, even in parks, consist of more than 3 to 4 percent bulls five years of age and older, simply because the rut is so hard on herd bulls.

paused for a brief moment and slid back to earth. If I'd blinked twice I might have missed it, but it's the standard mating method among elk. The bulls are often twice the size of the cows, and occasionally actually knock the cow to the ground.

Smaller satellite bulls looking to cut in on part of this action often keep the herd bull so busy that he doesn't get much breeding done, especially in populations with very high bull-to-cow ratios.

That same fall at the Bison Range I watched a herd bull with a dozen cows try to fend off nine smaller bulls. The satellites kept circling the herd, and the big bull was constantly on the run from one side of his harem to the other, chasing off smaller bulls. Some of them weren't much smaller, though, and I suspect that before long, some of the harem would end up in the hands—excuse me, hooves—of one or two of the satellites.

The tendency among herd bulls is, of course, to gather up as many cows as they can. The more a bull breeds, the more of his DNA he leaves in the population, and the more successful the young are biologically.

But harems are often simply too big. That bull with 29 cows, calves and one spike was about as big as I've seen, but another harem Eileen and I hunted late one September in the Gallatin Range was almost as large, at least for the first couple of days. Every other day, this herd of elk fed on the alfalfa fields of a rancher we knew. That's right, every other day. The elk bedded high on the north slope of the mountain behind the ranch, three or four miles from the alfalfa, and evidently didn't find it worth the effort to make the round-trip every night. But on even-numbered evenings they'd trek down the mountainside, graze on still-growing hay all night, then head up the mountain again.

It would seem that sitting in a tree-stand next to the hayfield would have been the logical way to put an arrow in an elk—except for one small factor. These were edge-of-civilization bulls, hunted constantly by all the rancher's friends, and the rancher's son's friends. The bulls knew that daylight meant people, so they started back up the mountain before shooting light.

In healthy elk herds, each harem is also followed at a discreet distance by lesser-ranking "satellite" bulls. Satellites often do manage to breed with a few cows—either when the herd bull is distracted by another satellite, or by stealing a few after the herd bull wears down over the several weeks of the rut.

DAILY ROUTINE of AN EARLY-FALL ELK HERD

Elk—and many other prey species—prefer to travel with the wind at their backs. That way they can see anything ahead of them (elk have very good eyesight) and smell anything behind. And a lot of elk herds, left undisturbed, are almost as habitual as farmland whitetails; witness that big harem I hunted for three days. They will bed up there, and feed down here, and you'll often find trails like cowpaths in between, rank with the barnyard smell of elk. In fact, I have shown innocent friends such paths, which they thought were made by Herefords or Angus until I pointed out that beef cows leave big cow pies, while elk leave cherry-sized droppings or, when feeding on very green food, small elk pies.

Wilderness herds often drop down a mountain with the cool down-canyon winds of evening and will feed until the sun rises in the morning. When the warm air begins rising up the canyons, the elk drift uphill with the wind at their backs, to their daytime bedding grounds in the shady timber.

But this civilized herd knew that people would be bugging them long before sunrise. They'd start up the mountain in the dark, their faces into any slight downhill

It's difficult to approach a bull elk with a harem, with so many additional pairs of eyes watching from every direction.

Eyes, Ears and Noses

Like most open-country herbivores, elk have excellent eyesight, the better to see predators. Also like other prey species, their eyes are set more toward the sides of their heads than those of predators such as wolves and humans. While elk do have binocular vision (where both eyes can focus on the same object) for about a 50-degree angle in front, the animals can all view an ever-wider angle with each eye individually. Consequently, their eyes are designed to perceive movement quite well but they don't discern stationary detail as well as do the eyes of humans and some other

predators. Like other deer, elk also have more light-sensitive but essentially color-blind "rod" cells in their eyes, allowing them to see quite well in low light and at night.

Elk also have fine hearing, but it doesn't tend to protect herd elk as much as it does single or small-group elk, such as mature bulls hiding out after the rut. A herd of elk is a noisy congregation. They "talk" a lot to each other, the short calf-chirps and cow-meows often erupting into a minute or more of almost constant sound. Their digestive systems are so large, and their relatively rough diet so hard to break down, that

even dull-eared humans can often hear a herd's stomachs rumbling from 100 yards away.

And elk are big animals, so they make a lot of noise simply walking around. In the timber they often break branches from deadfall while wandering back and forth feeding. Because of all the noise elk make, many hunters find it much easier to approach them than it is to approach most other Western big game, partly because elk themselves are so insensitive to the sound of breaking twigs or other "natural" forest noises.

Their hooves often make enough noise to be heard even when they're

Some big game animals depend more on one sense than another, but there's relatively little weakness in an elk's three primary senses: sight, hearing and smell.

breeze, which allowed them to smell any half-smart human sitting in a tree-stand. Sunrise usually found them about a half-mile up the mountain, entering the timber—Douglas fir and lodgepole pine broken by a few patches of quaking aspens. The trick was to try to catch the moving elk from the side, sneaking up on them in a cross-breeze. We tried this, and sometimes it almost worked.

One morning Eileen and I circled the face of a ridge just inside the timber, coming in alongside the herd's normal path. Fifteen minutes before legal shooting light, we stood on an old logging road, catching our breath.

After a minute or so, I bugled the thin whistle of a young bull. Immediately a big bull bellowed from the timber to our right, so close we could hear the wheeze at the beginning of his call. And then another bull sounded off in front of us, apparently from a meadow just on the edge of the timber, surrounded on the downhill side by a line of alders along a small stream. I cow-called once, and the bull above us bugled again, but he'd moved toward the meadow. Evidently that was where the center of the action was.

We walked the old road slowly and

trying to walk quietly on thick pine-needle duff. Fifteen years ago, when my hearing was better, I could often hear an elk approaching my call, the sound of its hooves resembling eggs falling from a few feet onto the forest floor, a soft, irregular thudding that once you've heard, you will always recognize. So when in herds, elk often make enough noise to cover the approach of a careful predator. But while alone, and bedded down in thick lodgepole, a big bull is almost impossible to approach on bare ground.

While you can fool elk eyes by standing very still, and elk ears are often overwhelmed by the noise of their herd-mates, elk noses are never fooled. Elk have very large nasal cavities, and the part of their brain that receives odors is highly developed. Elk seem able to detect the scent of humans at least as well as any bloodhound, which is strange because elk themselves are pretty smelly animals. I've often scented them myself, or even their empty bedding areas, sometimes from several hundred yards away (which is why you should always hunt elk into the wind whenever possible, rather than crosswind). A good whiff of barnyard odor means that

elk are in the area, which really helps when you're trying to sneak up on a herd. And as long as they don't smell you, even if you inadvertently startle a herd, it doesn't mean that the elk will leave.

Like many herd animals and flocking birds, elk begin to call and look for each other soon after the herd breaks up in a panic. On dry ground, some hunters even look for a bedded herd and will run into its midst, scattering elk in every direction, then cow-call to attract the herd's lonelier members. As long as they don't smell you, this tactic can and does work.

silently and reached the line of alders just at legal shooting light. We found a gap in the alders and eased through it, a step at a time, arrows nocked. The light was still very dim, the aspen leaves across the meadow, silvery in the predawn light, shimmered faintly in the light downhill breeze. And in the meadow stood a big bull elk, his pale side nearly colorless under the slight light of the sky. At least two dozen cows and calves surrounded him. His head was up and alert, and I decided to cow-call softly, to act as if we were a couple of his cows that had strayed into the alders along the tiny creek.

So I did, my lips almost closed. The head of every cow in that herd lifted, looking our way, and almost as regimented as a flock of geese, they started toward us, necks stretched out, the bull in the lead. I had just about decided to ease my bow up very slowly and draw, when somewhere, high up the mountain, the sun must have touched the dark-green trees, warming them enough to start lifting the air uphill. The light breeze, which had until that moment been caressing our right cheeks, now cooled the backs of our necks, and in two seconds every elk in that herd was running for the aspens. And when they did, another big bull

came out of the alders to our right, chasing them, and then another came thumping across the meadow, following the second bull. Neither was quite as big as the herd bull, but they were both mature six-points, not gangly adolescent "raghorns." We could hear the herd and its eager followers crash through the timber for several hundred yards; and then we heard an occasional crack or thump for several minutes as they headed up the mountain to their bedding grounds on the north side of the ridge.

Wild elk typically feed in semi-darkness, moving into timber by dawn's early light.

NATURAL VS. HUNTED AND DOMESTIC BULLS

*I*n "natural" unhunted elk populations, mature bull-cow ratios tend to remain fairly low, often only three or four bulls of four or more years per 100 cows. The low ratio is attributed to high competition among big bulls, which results not only in more bulls being wounded or even killed during the rut, but also in the poor condition of the bulls going into winter.

In hunted herds, the overall bull-cow ratio may be higher; but older, truly mature bulls of four years and up may be very scarce, due to the high turnover of bulls, especially on hard-hunted public land.

During the rifle season, only brow-tined bulls are legal in a popular public mountain range near my home in Montana. Winter game surveys show that virtually every 2½-year-old bull, the age class that normally first grows tined antlers, is taken during hunting season. Only spikes survive, to become next fall's breeders—and hunting crop. (This is much like the Pennsylvania deer season, which takes places after the rut; almost all young bucks are taken, but the does are already pregnant, ready to produce next year's crop.)

In "ranch" elk, far more mature bulls survive, mostly because fighting during the rut is minimized. This is either done by segregating mature bulls into separate pastures before the rut, or by cutting off most of the bulls' antlers for velvet. De-antlered bull elk don't fight antlered elk, even during the rut.

DIVORCE, ELK-STYLE

We went fishing for a day, then got up early the next day and again tried to intercept our big harem. Eileen and I split up that morning. She picked a stand along their path, the location a little too good. A herd of about six cows with one big bull walked right to her. As the lead cow passed on the upwind side of the tree, Eileen drew her bow, only to have the rest of the herd start barking in alarm as they walked on the downwind side. Elk again went crashing up the mountain.

In the meantime I saw another small harem-herd, with another big bull, walk up a draw ahead of me, and another friend hunting closer to the alfalfa fields saw yet a third harem with the original herd bull. Evidently in the confusion when we'd spooked them two days before, each of the other six-points had made off with part of the biggest bull's huge harem.

Eileen and I tracked "her" herd over a ridge to a big aspen thicket, where the herd had stopped to regroup. We stood silently on the hill above them and after a few minutes could hear the meows of mature cows and the shorter chirps of calves. I was just about to start cow-calling, hoping to pull either the bull or one of his harem closer, when another hunter on the ridge behind us let loose with a contest-winning bellow of a herd bugle. All we heard after that was the occasional soft thump of a hoof as the whole herd, probably pushed by their master, eased out of the aspens and up the ridge beyond. When they run they make as much noise as a car wreck, but when they sneak away, even two dozen elk are quieter than a single pine squirrel.

This constant shifting and running lasts for the rest of the rut. Sometimes, if the herds don't get startled by hunters, two big bulls will indeed fight—and seriously.

A bull bugling next to his harem will often gather his cows and disappear if challenged by a nearby bugle, whether made by an elk or a human.

76

But the antlers of elk, like those of many deer, were designed through evolution to "catch" the antlers of other elk rather than to be used as serious harem-fight weapons. This doesn't mean that bull elk don't injure or even kill each other during the rut. They are incredible fighting machines, pumped up by testosterone and adrenaline.

BULLS ON THE PROD

O ne of the likeliest places to see an elk fight each fall is the area in and around Mammoth, Wyoming, near the north entrance to Yellowstone Park. Elk move into the area late in summer, mostly because of the sprinkler-green lawns around the homes and Park Service buildings of Mammoth.

One late September day I watched as a herd bull and his harem took up residence in the front yards of three houses along a side street. As mentioned earlier, elk that eat fresh green feed leave frequent elk pies, and one home-dweller, evidently hoping to enjoy a peaceful day off, kept running out to his front yard with his shovel to chase elk away and to scoop up their latest deposits. Why was he liv-

ing in Yellowstone if elk and elk manure offended him so much?

But he was also lucky. Every fall, Mammoth elk watchers get chased up trees and back into their vehicles when some herd bull takes offense at their attentions. There are signs all over the place, and usually a ranger or two, warning people to stay away from rutting bulls, but evidently Americans are too used to seeing their nature on TV, where it's all benign and prepackaged. Every year somebody almost gets a free ride on a royal bull's brown tines.

And almost every year, fights break out among the bulls. The preliminaries involve some posturing, each bull tilting his antlers up to make them look larger, and flaring the hair on his neck and spine to make his body appear bigger. If something serious is about to happen, the two bulls (like many other deer) usually trot parallel to each other for 100 feet or more, posing sideways, their eyeballs white and glaring, before one bull suddenly breaks off the parallel-dance and charges the other.

The sound of four-foot antlers

Bull elk in rut don't truly fight very often, but when they do, they fight hard—and sometimes even chase humans.

clashing can be heard for half a mile on a calm day; after the antlers lock, the bulls mostly wrestle, heads down, pushing with their legs like draft horses pulling a covered wagon up Pike's Peak, twisting their heads trying to flip the other bull sideways. Most of the time that's all the fights amount to. But because of the length of elk antlers and tines, most bulls end up with dozens of wounds, especially around their necks and often on their rumps, inflicted when one bull breaks off and tries to run.

Sometimes one of the bulls does get another one down, at which point he tries to gore the fallen bull in the ribs. When a bull weighing almost half a ton puts all his weight behind his antlers, digs them into another bull's side, then pushes like a Holstein bull trying to break a gate, it seems impossible for the downed bull to survive. Even a big bull is only about 15 inches wide through the smallest part of the ribcage, and long tines of a mature elk can be even longer, able to punch through both lungs.

I have seen one unfortunate bull trip on a big sagebrush while being pushed backward in a fight, and be gored for several long minutes—the conquering bull giving him another deep thrust every time he even moved his legs—then get up and walk away after the other bull thought him dead. I don't know if the beaten bull survived for long, but he looked okay as he walked over the ridge, without even a limp.

When two well-matched bulls meet during the rut, they usually pose first, trying to impress one another with their antlers. If neither bull backs down, a real fight may take place.

Skinny, Wounded & Smelly Too

Such fighting and mating drains the herd bulls immensely during the month-long period between mid-September and mid-October. Often they'll lose 200 pounds or more during that period, their flesh so depleted of fat and eventually so full of lactic acid that it appears purplish rather than red. (As one bowhunter I know once said, "I'd rather eat a grizzly bear than an old blue-meated herd bull.")

Some of the wounds on a bull's neck will become infected and drip pus. Add to this his frequent baths in urine-fouled wallows. A mature bull in mid-October can look pitiful, with hipbones often showing through rump-skin that was stretched taut by fat only a month earlier, and he can be smelled for hundreds of yards, even by the "scent-deaf" noses of humans.

How long the bulls keep rutting depends on several factors. Most of the cows bred during the two-week peak are mature, but younger cows

and even calves can come into estrus after the first mature cows. I've often seen herd bulls, both in Yellowstone and on publicly hunted National Forest land, actively herding and even breeding cows during the last half of October.

Montana's general rifle season opens on the fourth Sunday in October, somewhere around the 22nd to 25th most years, and quite a few herd bulls meet a .30-06 bullet then because they're still bugling, somewhat hoarsely and half-heartedly. The latest I ever heard a bull bugle was on November 15th, while hunting deer in the Bull Mountains of central Montana. The Bulls are almost all on private land,

Bulls are often injured and sometimes even killed during rut fights. This old bull will have a tough time making it through the winter after injuring an eye; predators will be able to sneak up on his blind side.

and not really mountains but piney breaks, too easily hunted to allow a general rifle season for elk. So only a few are taken there each year, by bowhunters and the few rifle hunters lucky enough to draw a permit. Consequently, there are lots of avail-able cows for each bull, so some of the females don't breed during their first estrus. This causes the breeding season to extend later in the fall, when the cows come into heat again about 28 days after their first cycle. If they do, the bulls are still ready.

Bulls often urinate and wallow in small seeps or pools during the rut, covering themselves in stinking mud. This seems to cool the bull as well as attract females.

Tree Rubs and Wallows

When elk antlers harden in August, bulls spend considerable time rubbing them on small saplings, especially conifers. This may help scrape the now-dead velvet from the hard bone under-neath, but some biologists point out that velvet contains more oil than any other skin on an elk's body, so bull elk may also be leaving their scent as a sign to cows. And even after the velvet is long gone from their antlers, bulls attack saplings, especially young, limber lodgepole pines. In fact, during the pre-rut, an abundance of freshly "skinned" saplings is one sure sign that bulls are in the area, and they often return to rub young trees in the same area year after year.

An angry bull, usually one challenged by another, often takes his aggression out by beating up young and innocent pine trees, so some of the behavior is also probably testosterone-induced aggression. If a bull happens to break off a branch or even a whole pine, he'll often wear it proudly in his antlers to exaggerate his rack's size.

A rutting bull also seeks out water. Some of this is just because he's thirsty; courting cows and chasing away other bulls on September afternoons is hard work. But a bull will also look for a small, shallow, water-filled depression such as a puddle made by a spring or a drying pothole. Bulls urinate in the water, then tear up the puddle floor with their antlers, creating a stinking mud-pie that they then roll in, like

WINDING DOWN . . . JUST IN TIME

In most populations the herd bulls leave the cows sometime in late October. It was once thought that the bulls left the prime feed for the cows, allowing the females to feed well to support their growing fetuses, but recent research indicates the opposite.

Instead of offering coarser, inferior feed, the smaller back-country

Thin and half-blind after the rut, this bull probably won't survive much beyond the first snows.

a dog rolling in dead fish. Such "wallows" are another sure sign that bull elk old enough to hold harems are in the area and, like herds of elk, these wallows can often be smelled for several hundred yards.

Big bulls also urinate all over their bellies, necks and faces, directing the stream quite accurately from their flexible, controllable penises. Often they urinate over their belly in spurts as they grunt after bugling. The urine contains many subtle smells that we can't discern, scents both of sex hormones and fat that's being broken down as a bull enters full rut. The hormones help attract cows, and the fat content tells the cows about the bull's health. A lot of fat in his urine, like a lot of antler on his head, means that a bull has eaten well over the summer and that he will be good genetic material for the calf that, at the moment, is only a maniacal gleam in his mud-rimmed eyes.

meadows where rut-weak bulls feed often offer higher-calorie food than the big meadows where the cow herds live. The cows can exist on such coarser food because they haven't been as depleted by the rut. Their better condition and abundant companions provide protection from predators even in open country.

But the bulls seek out thick timber near small, good-forage meadows, often higher up the mountain, where they can rest and eat and replenish their energy and lick their wounds. Their level of testosterone drops again, and they now find other bulls acceptable company again, though you won't normally find the large bachelor groups that are common in late summer. Normally no more than a pair of bulls hangs out together, for the excellent reason that their small food-sources can't take much grazing. Even rutted-out bulls will weigh 750 pounds and require a lot of food if they're going to recover enough to live out the winter.

After the rut, bull elk often retreat to thicker cover to rest and recover. All they require is a small meadow and, in dry autumns, a seep of water.

WHEN NOT TO BUGLE

Many bulls don't make it much past the rut. If humans can smell a stinking October bull for several hundred yards, how far can a wolf pack or grizzly bear smell one? Many rut-weakened bulls fall to predators, even before recovery can begin. In fact, one reason that many bowhunters refuse to bugle anymore in certain parts of Montana, Idaho and Wyoming is that grizzly bears sometimes key on elk bugles, especially later in the rut when a bull is weakened and perhaps even by himself, still looking for one last cow in heat.

My friend Bill McRae, the well-known wildlife photographer, was once bowhunting along the Rocky Mountain Front in Montana, one of the wildest areas left in the Lower 48, home to every big game animal that lived in the state when Lewis and Clark came through, from grizzlies and wolves to mountain goats and white-tailed deer. Bill was easing along the edge of some timber, bugling occasionally, trying to locate

Rut-weakened bull elk often fall prey to large predators, including bears, mountain lions, wolves ... and humans.

a bull, when suddenly he heard a big animal running toward him. Its feet didn't thump as hard as an elk's though, and Bill barely had time to get the call out of his mouth when a huge, almost-black boar grizzly bear came charging right toward him.

For bear protection, Bill had a .44 Mag. revolver on his hip as well as some capsicum bear spray, but didn't have time to use either. The only reason he survived, Bill says, is because the bear realized he wasn't an elk and, on its last bound, turned slightly away. As the bear sailed by him, like a lion jumping through a hoop in the circus and just about as close, it turned and looked Bill in the eyes before landing

and running off into the timber again. Bill says he did not hunt any more that day, and never uses a bugle when hunting elk anymore. In fact, I do not believe he bowhunts along the Front anymore, instead preferring the rifle season when he can carry a heavier, more quickly available rifle.

Mature post-rut bulls are not only killed by bears and wolves, but are even killed by mountain lions. In fact, a rutted-out bull elk can be favored prey among mature lions.

When I was a wildlife biology student at the University of Montana in the 1970s, one of my fellow students was studying lions. Back then, mountain lions were still a wilderness animal for a couple of reasons: There just weren't as many of the big cats around, and fewer people had built ranchettes up every little side-canyon of the West, invading their territory. My friend radio-collared and tracked lions all year round, from late October on; he found numbers of lion-killed bull elk and buck mule deer, usually mature animals. Most of these were killed by one lion—from the size of the tracks, a large male.

Today, with the mountain lion populations high across most of the West, young lions searching for new territory, and subdivisions creeping up many canyons, mountain lions have expanded their autumn menu from elk and deer to poodles, llamas and even the occasional human.

One study found that mountain lions often prey on mature bull elk after the rut. Post-rut bulls often live alone at high elevations, making them more susceptible to high-country cats.

Even Bull Elk Get the Blues

These post-rut bulls are very weak. I've found quite a few in Yellowstone, bedded in thick lodgepole timber. Unlike some of the wildlife photographers (as well as the "wannabes" and amateurs) who invade the park each fall, I am quite a bit more courteous to a beat-up, plumb-tired bull. As soon as these bulls notice me, I stop. From then on, I take any photo from a distance with a long telephoto lens. The last thing a nicked-up, gaunt, late-October bull needs is to be forced to his feet by some pushy human shutterbug.

The cows, on the other hand, are now having a fine time. The calves they suckled all summer have now been weaned, and they have nothing to do but eat and grow the new calf inside their belly. Unwounded and still fat from a summer of green meadows, they now find the frost-cured grass of the same meadows plenty to live on, and quite palatable too, at least until the deep snows of winter begin to fall. ✳

Almost devoid of body fat, bull elk move as little as possible after the rut. Unless heavy snows force them to migrate to lower elevations with the cows, bulls sometimes remain in the same area for months, rebuilding their worn bodies.

Part Two

WINTER

WILD HAY

January 22. This noon I went out to the Elk Refuge and helped the boys load hay. Just as we finished, a bunch of elk came right up to the hay shed. Another stormy day, the air thick with snow; it is almost impossible to see where you are going. The elk were plastered with snow: on their faces, necks, and along their sides; surely a storm-driven lot.

We went out with our loads of hay and the elk lined out, feeding greedily, fighting over it, running here and there for a new supply. Repeatedly big bulls rose on their hind legs and boxed each other; two spikes and cows did also. In the storm I began to see little mounds, like snowy hummocks, and realized these were dead calves, drifted over. One was lying with its head tucked in under its flank; still alive, but barely so. A forkful of hay was thrown to him, but he gave no heed. Other elk gathered about it and cheerfully ate the hay. The calf was too far gone to care; it had lost interest and had turned its head away from all earthly things. Ravens stood in a group a distance away. They had sized up the situation.

—Margaret and Olaus Murie,
Wapiti Wilderness, *1966*

Margaret and Olaus Murie lived in many places during Olaus's career with the United States Biological Survey, the government agency that eventually became the U.S. Fish and Wildlife Service. But they lived the longest in

Elk seek out areas where wind blows away snow during winter, or lower elevations where snow normally doesn't pile so deeply.

the beautiful valley called Jackson Hole in Wyoming, where Olaus did the research for his book, *The Elk Of North America*, the first intensive look at the life-cycle of "wapiti."

Jackson Hole was originally settled in the 1880s, later than much of the West, primarily because of its high elevation. The town of Jackson lies slightly more than 6,200 feet above sea level, too high to grow corn or wheat or other traditional farm crops (though Hollywood didn't care, filming the western *Shane* in the valley, a classic story of homesteading farmers vs. free-range cattlemen).

But Jackson Hole and other high-elevation valleys along the spine of the Rockies, like Montana's Big Hole, do grow one natural crop: hay.

The flat valley floors often have rich soil, a combination of glacial till and outwash from the mountains. The valleys also have lots of water, a rarity in the West and the result of a combination of natural factors. First, high mountains, like the Tetons above Jackson Hole and like the

Valley bottoms are normally covered with less snow, making finding food easier. Plus, temperatures are milder lower down, allowing elk to preserve calories necessary for survival.

Bitterroots above the Big Hole, catch lots of snow during winter. Then the very short sub-alpine summers don't allow much evaporation of the melting snow. The flat valley floor essentially "swims" barely above the water table all summer long; the abundant groundwater feeds not only hundreds of springs but also the roots of wild grasses and sedges, all fertilized by the rich soil.

Before alfalfa came to the West, wild Big Hole hay was exported to Kentucky to feed thoroughbreds. Soon after settlement, Jackson Hole hay fed beef cattle on the ranches that eventually almost covered the valley.

CATTLE RANCHING VS. ELK

There was only one problem with Jackson Hole ranching. Or, maybe it's more accurate to say there were thousands of problems: the thousands of elk that had lived in the mountains around the valley since the last Ice Age. They lived there because of the valley's wild hay, that rich and abundant food that allowed them to live through subzero winters.

But after white people began ranching the valley, the elk's winter rations started to disappear. Instead of growing tall each summer and fall-curing on the stem, ready for the mouths of wild wapiti, more and more of Jackson Hole's wild hay was being swathed and stacked, and what wasn't cut was grazed all summer by cattle.

The inevitable happened: A really hard winter came along in 1889 and elk began to starve.

Some elk found ranchers' haystacks and were shot. Others, easy prey in the deep snow, were killed for their tusks. Eight years later came another bad winter, with similar results. Residents of the area started asking for help for the elk, so in 1905 the state of Wyoming stepped in and established the Teton Game Preserve, protecting part of the valley for "winter range" and outlawing hunting on the preserve.

In winter, elk often move into foothill cattle pastures, creating conflicts with ranching.

But it wasn't quite enough. Elk were becoming scarce throughout North America, and something had to be done to protect the few thousand that were left. Consecutive severe winters in 1909 and 1910 killed even more elk, so the federal government stepped in and established the National Elk Refuge just outside of the town of Jackson in 1912.

The Game Preserve and Elk Refuge still didn't provide enough winter range for the Jackson Hole elk herd, so some of the hay was cut to feed elk in winter. The practice still goes on today, and elk-feeding is one of Jackson's more popular winter sights enjoyed by skiers and other visitors.

Thousands of elk winter on the Refuge each year, and are fed hay from sleds. When I lived in Wyoming in the early 1970s, several of us took a sleigh-ride tour of the elk grounds, seeing the same fighting over food that the Muries observed. Anybody who really believes wild animals—even herbivores like elk—live peaceably together, like the biblical lion and lamb, should take a winter sleigh ride on the Jackson feeding grounds.

Elk are large and fertile animals with hearty appetites, so pretty soon there were too many elk coming to eat the hay each winter in Jackson Hole. Some were trapped and given away, along with elk gathered off the high plateaus of Yellowstone Park. Some were shipped to rather unsuitable places such as the state of Louisiana and the Park Commission in Canton, Ohio. Others ended up with the Buenos Aires Zoological Gardens and on several ranches in Mexico. But most of the elk were restocked in other Rocky Mountain states where the animals were scarce or had disappeared entirely. In fact, almost all the elk that today exist in the Rockies and plains states, from Arizona north to Alberta, are descendants of the Jackson Hole and Yellowstone herds.

Even winter range sometimes isn't the most hospitable environment for January elk, especially in the northern Rockies.

ELK & CATTLE

While elk can and do compete, at least marginally, with other grazing animals, they have the most conflicts with domestic cattle, and for one simple reason: Elk and cattle have very similar food preferences. So cattle ranchers in general don't like elk, which is only fair since elk in general don't like cattle.

Most studies show that elk don't like to hang around cattle during warmer months, perhaps because cattle are larger and more used to being crowded, so they tend to dominate elk. On winter range, however, much of this intolerance disappears, probably because hungry elk have no choice.

In much of elk country, competition between the two is actually not great. Except in winter, cattle tend to feed along bottomlands while elk graze steeper slopes. Cattle are also normally fenced inside a certain pasture at any given time of year, while elk can easily jump the typical barbed-wire cattle fence. Cattle need more water than elk, so they tend to hang around streams or wells even after the prime forage is grazed off, while elk will move along, looking for better eating.

The primary competition comes during winter, when pastures are limited. The cold months are also when elk are likely to raid haystacks, which does not endear them to ranchers trying to feed Angus or Herefords through winter. But as I noted elsewhere, several studies have shown that carefully timed cattle grazing can actually benefit elk range; the elk will typically graze the same area later in the year, when the cows have been moved to lower-elevation winter pastures.

Usually it's not direct competition for food, however, that gets ranchers mad at elk. It's the damage they do to fences. Elk can jump any fence up to about 8 feet high—and if they can't jump it, it had better be strong, because otherwise they'll break it down.

Elk are particularly hard on barbed-wire gates. Despite their leaping ability, elk naturally look for low places to jump fences, allowing them to use less energy. Gates are typically lower, and the wire often looser. An elk herd will jump a gate one at a time, the smaller elk often striking the top of the gate. By the time the twentieth elk has leaped over, the top strand or one of the end-posts is often broken, or the gate simply collapses because of the stretched wire.

I once spent a couple of autumns guiding hunters on several ranches in the breaks along the Musselshell River in south-central Montana, where elk had recently migrated from a nearby mountain range. The outfitter I worked for received angry phone calls constantly from a couple of the ranchers he leased hunting rights from, accusing his damn guides of not closing gates after they drove through, or even driving right over the gates instead of opening them properly. It took some convincing to persuade those ranchers that elk were breaking his gates, but after they realized what was happening, we never had any trouble taking elk hunters onto those ranches. In fact, we sometimes got phone calls telling us exactly where the elk were hanging out.

HOW CAN THERE BE TOO MANY ELK?

lk make one of the finest success stories in American conservation. In fact, they are becoming almost too successful in many places. Elk are now so abundant across much of the West that some states sell resident hunters a second, "antlerless" elk tag each year. But the problem won't be alleviated soon, because smaller, private

The first heavy snows and deep cold can drive elk suddenly downhill in large herds, determined to reach traditional winter range. Such migrations sometimes leave elk "roads" 100 feet wide.

versions of the National Elk Refuge are cropping up all over the West.

Elk are not only large and fertile, but are true herd animals with long memories. Led by the older cows, herds head for traditional wintering grounds soon after the first significant snowfall. It's surprising how a little early snow will bring elk down out of the high mountains. My friend, occasional hunting partner and elk nut Jay Rightnour puts it succinctly: "When compared to mule deer, elk are wimps." He's partially right, and for excellent biological reasons.

Deep snow covers most grass (i.e., food) and also makes traveling difficult. Elk trapped by sudden snowfall often can't migrate out of mountain canyons, and entire herds may die.

Since elk are such large animals, and have evolved in cool to cold climates, they have a relatively low tolerance for heat and a much larger tolerance for cold. But even elk in their winter coats can be chilled.

When arctic fronts lash their way south across the Rockies, bringing subzero temperatures, snow and wind, elk often head for what biologists term "cold thermal cover." This is usually very thick brush or timber, often on the lee side of a ridge. Thickly growing conifers, like young lodgepole pine thickets (the familiar "doghair" of the serious elk hunter), are often chosen.

These thickets help in two ways: they provide overhead cover, which helps keep snow off the elks' backs and their body heat from rising into the open sky; and they prevent convective heat loss from cold wind. Without adequate and effective thermal cover, elk use many calories just keeping their bodies warm, and they tend to lose weight rapidly even when eating prime winter-range grass or even second-cut alfalfa hay. Lack of thermal cover can limit elk numbers even on good winter range.

Oddly enough, in the very coldest weather, cold thermal cover can be in almost exactly the same places as shaded summer thermal cover: the north slopes of ridges. Timber grows most thickly on shaded north slopes, and thick timber provides the most effective protection against both extreme heat and cold.

ELK IN LATE AUTUMN

The first snows usually find elk well-scattered in elevation. A few will be found hanging along foothills, creekbottoms, near abundant water with its lush riparian grass and, often, near the crops of farms and ranches. But most elk will have been pushed higher not only by bowhunters and ranchers protecting their hayfields, but also by a typical late-summer drought that dries up the foothills' grass. Many elk will hide in mid-elevation canyons, halfway up the mountains. Other elk, usually the mature bulls, range higher yet—sometimes up along the edge of timberline—feeding off little meadows bounded by rocky slopes that look more like bighorn sheep country than elk habitat.

These mountain elk are first pushed to the low country by early, wet snows that cover the frost-cured grass.

Before the first deep snows of late autumn, elk live anywhere they can find food, cover and respite from hunters. The herds can be widely scattered and hard to find.

Unlike low-country grasses, many Western grasses, adapted to higher elevations, react well to early cold: The first frosts preserve rather than destroy much of their nutritional value. So elk continue to feed on them as long as snow doesn't cover them. These elk gain weight, even after the first cold nights of September.

But wet snow turns this short, natural hay unpalatable, at least temporarily, so even four inches of sloppy October flakes will push many elk downhill, looking for still-green grass along creeks, or for alfalfa that's grown a few inches since its final cutting, or for sprouts of winter wheat.

Jay knows all about this because he lives three miles from the foothills of the Big Belt Mountains. His house looks down on a trout stream and backs against a juniper-sagebrush hillside that soon levels out into the wheat- and hayfields owned by a rancher neighbor. Finger draws filled with juniper and ponderosa pine divide the fields, and as soon as the first significant snow falls, Jay starts to look for elk and elk tracks.

The elk usually show up in the cottonwoods along the trout creek below his house, but they rarely stay there long, since most of the creek-bottom is visible from the state highway paralleling the stream. Soon they cross the highway and head up the conifered draws behind Jay's house, bedding there during the day and feeding in the fields during late evening and early morning.

Jay waits until he finds fresh tracks crossing the road, then calls in at work and takes the next day off. It is still understood in parts of the West that "getting your elk" is just as important as taking your kids to the

Snow brings elk downhill to where hunters can more easily locate them, and sometimes even brings the animals right into town.

county rodeo or celebrating the Fourth of July. In short, it is the America of 50 or 100 years ago, which a lot of urbanized America cannot understand.

Some years, Jay just calls and says his elk is at the meat-cutter's, but once in a great while I help him load a bull into the back of his pick-up. It is kind of odd to someone who grew up when elk were, if not rare, still a hard-won part of November. Elk hunting in the 1960s called for tough climbs in shin-high snow, and long drags back down the mountain, slowed by elk quarters. But in the 1990s I have stood in wheat-stubble, heaving one of Jay's elk up on the tailgate, and heard the whine of commuter tires on the cold asphalt of the highway a few hundred yards away.

Several studies have quantified what serious elk hunters have known for decades: Elk don't like roads. One study found that more than one mile of publicly open road in each section of land (a square mile) tended to drive elk away and also that elk herds tended to live on the other side of any ridge from a road. There are lots of reasons for this, ranging from poaching, the dogs that often accompany humans in the woods, or simply a woodland creature's innate dislike of any disturbance.

But it is a trend I've seen over the decades, and one that's heatedly debated all over the West. Each year, various government agencies and many private conservation groups try to lock up more roadless country, prevent the building of new roads or even destroy old roads. Many local hunters protest these actions, feeling that fewer roads blocks access to anybody without horses or extremely strong legs. Both sides have points, and no study that I've seen has shown that elk thrive better in completely roadless country, such as federally designated Wilderness Areas. In fact, because such areas are often off-limits to controlled logging, fewer elk live there, because large expanses of mature forests don't provide much elk food.

Of course, there's logging and then there's logging. Small clearcuts on relatively level ground help most large animals, from deer to grizzly bears, because of the abundant food growing on the newly opened ground. But only if the road in

doesn't remain open, allowing anybody to drive right up to the clearcut and lean a .300 magnum out the window. (Yes, this does happen, despite the practice being generally illegal, and is one of the reasons elk avoid roads.) But huge "scalping" clearcuts don't do the land any good, especially for wildlife, since other studies have shown that game animals rarely feed more than 100 yards from the edge of the timber and that such huge cuts really allow land to erode.

I do most of my own elk hunting on public U.S. Forest Service land that's been

logged in the past 20 years, in which small clearcuts that attract deer and elk have been created. But the old logging roads have been closed, so I have to park down in the valley, by a locked gate, and hike up there. This really isn't too tough, even for an elk hunter pushing 50, and closed Forest Service roads allow the use of wheeled carts in dry weather, and plastic toboggans on snow, to bring out elk quarters.

So roads can be both a blessing and a curse to elk and elk hunters. Roads accompanied by small, controlled clearcuts provide food for elk and provide places for hunters to find elk during autumn. But when too many roads or huge clearcuts scar the land, both elk and elk hunters lose.

Elk are true creatures of the wilderness. Too many roads, and the excessive motorized and human traffic they bring, drive elk deeper into our ever-shrinking backcountry.

THE MODERN EQUIVALENT OF THE OLD FRONTIER

The highway running through Jay's elk-hunting territory is unfortunate, but this is the modern West, and human civilization is an essential part of elk biology today. One of the reasons we have more and more elk every year, despite long hunting seasons that last from the bugling time of September through the snows of January, is that many citizens of the new West have created miniature versions of the National Elk Refuge.

Some of these are simply subdivisions, planted right in the middle of elk winter range. I'll describe winter range here, so you can understand the problem.

"Winter range" in the 21st century is not exactly what it was in the early 19th century. As soon as transplanted Europeans and their descendants "settled" the West, most of the wide-open valleys like Jackson Hole were no longer winter range, for elk or any other wildlife. Instead, winter range became the foothills above the valleys, where cured wild grass grew between aspen-bordered streams and under scattered sagebrush sidehills that backed against the steeper, conifered slopes at the base of the mountains. Here elk could bed in the timber, whether aspen or pine, and feed on the wind-blown grassy ridges or sagebrush "parks." As the prime valley bottomland was turned into towns, or irrigated hayfields, some farmers and ranchers found they could grow hay or even grain on the foothill benches, adding to the elk's winter larder.

But as many people living in the bal-

looning cities on our coasts grew tired of traffic and crime, and of living in apartments or houses built window-to-window, and as new technologies helped more people make a living wherever they wanted to live, many folks came Out West for a piece of the wilderness and a little elbow room.

In the meantime, many longtime ranchers found themselves making less

This bull is lying peacefully in short grass on winter range. Unfortunately, human encroachment into the wilderness and semi-wilderness has fragmented, and even eliminated, much valuable winter elk range.

*I*n all but the mildest winters, elk herds in the northern Rockies can suffer severe winter mortality rates. Most elk die during late winter, because the built-up months of cold have sapped their bodies of reserve strength. One Wyoming study analyzed bone marrow fat from yearling cows. The researcher rated a fat content of 80 to 100 percent as excellent. Over the midwinter months, most of the elk still had "excellent" amounts of fat in their marrow, but by March none did.

Older cows tend to have more fat reserves, partly because they've learned where the best food can be found over the seasons. But they also stop growing after four years of age; the summer food they eat doesn't have to grow as much bone and muscle, so it builds more fat. Older cows are much larger, which helps them retain body heat; a big cow can weigh more than 600 pounds, not much smaller than a mature bull.

Bulls quit growing after five years, but after that they're the center of the rut's frenzy, which sucks fat from their bodies. Cow elk up to 10 years of age have plenty of fat content in their bodies, but bulls more than seven years old tend to have lower fat content, the result of rut stress. Consequently, bulls tend to die sooner than cows, and bulls from unhunted populations also suffer higher mortality rates. The higher bull-cow ratio creates more stress during the rut, and the larger-bodied bulls need to eat more, especially during the tough-forage winter months, which increases tooth wear. Eventually, like old men, old bulls just can't chew tough food very well anymore, and sooner or later don't make it through winter.

So more bulls and calves tend to die than mature cows during most winters, another result of evolution. Breeding-age females are always the most important part of any animal population; without them the species will perish. Since it only takes a few bull elk to impregnate lots of cows, bulls become expendable after the rut. And during a long, cold winter, some preadolescents are also expendable, since they compete directly for food with pregnant cows. This goes against the human belief that children should be saved before adults— which is also probably natural, rising from the long period of nurturing and protection that human young require before reaching adolescence.

But if a bunch of men, women and children were caught on a sinking ship with only one lifeboat, the rational way to preserve Homo sapiens, not just in that moment of crisis but for future generations, would be to throw the kids overboard, along with all but a few of the men. And that's exactly how Rocky Mountain elk preserve *Cervus elaphus canadensis* while the ship of life sinks over a long winter.

of a living, because of various factors including, but not limited to, imports of foreign cattle, a general notion that cattle grazing on public land is not desirable (many of the foothill ranches also graze cattle on the public U.S. Forest Service land above them), and more coyotes, mountain lions and, sometimes, wolves and grizzly bears, all of which have returned to the West in abundance since the settlement days, when they were generally shot and trapped as enemies of civilization, as they had been for millennia in Europe and Asia.

I am not trying to point any fingers here, just explaining the facts. Somehow the American West has become one of the great paradoxes of modern civilization, perceived as wilderness by many urban and suburban folks—who then think they can move Out West and buy up 5 or 10 or 20 acres of this wilderness and live free, like Elsa the lioness. Perhaps it is just the American myth of the endless frontier that has plagued us since Columbus accidentally hit San Salvador, the Daniel Boone notion that there's always free, "unruined" land over the next ridge.

The idea of endless, empty land is something that Europeans and Asians divested themselves of hundreds if not thousands of years ago, and despite the lessons that could be learned from their history, we Americans don't—or won't—listen.

As more and more winter range is taken by human development, more elk starve. Winter is hardest on mature bulls—who are thin and exhausted from the rut—and young calves.

MOVING ⚜ OLD WEST OUT

So we make it harder and harder for ranchers to earn a living, saying their way of life is antiquated, and then we not only continue to eat burgers and wear leather clothes, but we also eagerly buy up their ranches so we can plant them with non-native plants like Normandy poplars and Kentucky bluegrass, and populate them with foreign animals like poodles and llamas. We turn the foothills into ranchettes with spectacular views of the mountains and valley and 100 other ranchettes, then eagerly await the wildlife that come to visit. Until, of course, a mule deer eats our flowers or a mountain lion eats our poodle.

Do not get me wrong here. I count myself as an ardent hunter-environmentalist, the sort of person who, like Theodore Roosevelt, was called a hunter-naturalist a century ago. But the modern "environmental" movement often finds no place for people and their by-products in its vision of the wilderness, despite the word "environment," meaning "the world around us." So for years we heard slogans aimed at driving the cattle ranchers from the Wild West—like "No Moo By '92!" or "Beef Free By '93!"—all promoting the removal of the so-called free-loading ranchers from public lands.

But many ranchers have grown tired of urban animosity and are going broke, then selling the private part of their private/public ranch to ski resorts and subdividers. End result? We have even less open space than before. And the open space that gets "developed" is usually the most important part for Rocky Mountain wildlife: their winter home and pantry. I know people who belong to and even speak for large "conservation" organizations that built and live in huge houses right in the middle of prime winter range.

Enough preaching. But winter range development truly is one problem of the modern West, and it is growing worse. The elk "over-population" problem is not really one of too many elk. After all, North America still has only a fraction of the elk that existed here when the Pilgrims managed to avoid crashing into Plymouth Rock. The real problem is a shortage of places for elk to live. Right now they tend to spend winters on whatever ranch doesn't allow hunting. The herd of 200-odd wapiti living in a certain mountain canyon soon discovers that movie-star X's 1,000 acres of getaway do not get hunted at any time, or that the gentle tourists

Much elk winter range is private land, mostly ranches. If ranchers can't make a living, they sell out to land developers. While some elk can survive in subdivisions, more can exist in "undeveloped" country.

Aside from the fairly common pneumonia caused primarily by necrotic stomatitis, elk are often hosts to several parasites and often contract other diseases.

Ticks regularly attach themselves to elk, but only the winter tick seems to cause real weakening, mostly in Roosevelt elk and in southern Canadian Rocky Mountain herds.

As noted elsewhere, flies (particularly horseflies) and mosquitoes often drive elk off prime meadows during summer. Yearly weather conditions that breed lots of flies probably do affect elk going into fall.

ELK DISEASES
AND MORTALITY

Many elk carry the large liver fluke; in fact, elk imported to Europe have infected domestic cattle there, which causes real problems in beef herds. But the fluke doesn't seem to affect elk much, except to render the liver inedible to humans. (The carcass meat is fine.) Cow elk tend to be infected more than bulls, probably because they graze more on moist lowland meadows where the fluke can be passed on.

Some tapeworms and roundworms infest elk, but unless elk are already stressed by poor nutrition, neither has much effect.

The really deadly elk parasites are certain arterial worms and lungworms. Arterial worms evidently evolved in mule deer, and are often transferred by horseflies. So they infest elk most commonly in the southwest, where mule deer and elk frequent the same country during horsefly season. Horsefly worms don't have any noticeable debilitating effect on deer, but in elk the larvae block arteries in the head, often leading to blindness or brain damage, both eventually fatal. Overall, mule deer population trends have gone steadily downward since extremely high numbers in the 1950s, which may help explain why elk are increasing, especially in the Southwest.

Lungworms are also often carried harmlessly by deer—including whitetails, blacktails and mule deer—but affect the brain and spinal cord of elk, destroying nerve tissue. The abundant whitetail hosts in the eastern United States are one reason why eastern elk will probably always be very local, despite numerous attempts to reestablish populations.

The really big problems in elk disease are brucellosis and chronic wasting disease. Brucellosis is a special problem of the Yellowstone/Jackson herds, and the prime reason for the controversy over bison from Yellowstone leaving the park. Also known as Bang's disease and undulant fever, in humans it results in a particularly long-lasting, debilitating illness, characterized by bouts of fever, accompanied by exhaustion, joint pain and headaches. The symptoms ease for a few days, then recur, then dissipate again. This pattern keeps up, sometimes over months. Antibiotics can cure human brucellosis, but sometimes it takes a while to diagnose, and long-term cases can exacerbate arthritis later in life. My friend Jim Conley caught brucellosis from a wild pig in Florida, and says you do not ever want to contract a case of undulant fever.

Brucellosis also causes domestic cattle to abort their unborn calves. Because of both this and the danger of human infection, ranchers and livestock agencies strove for years to eradicate the disease in cattle herds, and have largely succeeded. To reinoculate herds that have been disease-free for generations is a very expensive process, and if a certain state's cattle aren't certified brucellosis-free, they can't be shipped out of state.

Both elk in the Yellowstone region and bison from the park regularly carry brucellosis. It doesn't affect them much, but ranchers around the Park are afraid that bison may infect cattle, the reason Western states (and especially Montana, to where most park bison migrate in winter) try to keep Yellowstone buffalo away from cattle range. In one bad winter year, this resulted in more than 1,000 buffalo being killed as they left the park.

Much controversy surrounds the issue: Bison proponents say there's no hard evidence that buffalo can pass the disease on, and killing any Park buffalo depletes the last gene pool of pure plains bison. But ranchers understandably want to be sure their herds aren't infected.

What's ignored in the whole controversy is that many Park elk carry the disease too. But there's no concerted effort to keep Yellowstone elk off surrounding ranches. What's the difference?

Bison are a charismatic symbol of several romantic things—a pristine America, the Plains Indians' supermarket, the last of the Pleistocene megafauna. And nobody hunts them, unlike the abundant elk that drift out of the park every year. If any rancher suggested that Yellowstone elk should be shot at the border to protect domestic Angus from brucellosis, they'd be ostracized, if not actually hung by a lynch mob. But if you ever hunt elk in the Yellowstone area, be aware that any elk you take may very well infect you with undulant fever. Once cooked, the meat's fine, but elk blood on any open wound can infect a hunter.

Chronic Wasting Disease (CWD) is another issue. First found in Colorado, it's been likened to mad cow disease, but is really only vaguely related. CWD does, however, kill elk and deer by slowly destroying their entire system. It may also infect humans, but the jury is still out on that. The major problem with CWD is that it is beginning to show up in game ranch elk; elk on a ranch in western Montana one fall were proven to be infected, so all of its 70-odd elk had to be destroyed.

The big problem is that at the moment, there's no positive test for CWD on live animals, so only carcasses can be tested—the reason the whole elk ranch herd had to be killed. The game ranching industry is regulated in very different ways across the country—in fact, fearing ranching will pass diseases to wild game, some states, including Wyoming, don't allow game ranching at all.

That was the fear in Montana. After the infected "tame" elk were killed, more than 30 elk and mule deer from the area surrounding the fenced-in ranch were killed and tested. None had CWD, but they very easily could have. Where did the infected elk come from? Were any sold to other elk ranchers? With "tame game" being shipped across the country more and more often these days, answers to those questions are vital to the health of wild elk and other native game all across the country.

at Elk Mountain Resort do not want their bottle of Cabernet Sauvignon and plate of "farm-raised" Norwegian salmon to be disturbed by the sound of .30-06s.

So in many areas it doesn't matter how much the state wildlife department tries to "use hunters as tools" to keep local elk herds at a sustainable level, where they don't overgraze what little winter-range is left or chomp on the haystacks of ranchers who haven't subdivided yet. A lot of elk in the New West are nearly unhuntable, spending their summers in inaccessible canyons, then making a beeline for some miniature elk refuge as soon as hunting season opens.

What all this means is that hunters will be taking more and more elk in untraditional ways. Jay Rightnour, with his next-to-the-highway elk, hunts behind his house. And my outfitter friend Tom Tietz, who lives in a Denver suburb, took a huge bull out of a foothills subdivision with his bow a few years ago. How long that kind of hunting will last is anybody's guess, as more and more people populate the West and perceive the Rockies as bisected either into wilderness museums or "view homes," leaving little room for hunting.

GOING UP ❧ COMING DOWN

So that is the nature of fall elk migrations in a large part of the West. In many ways, of course, it resembles the natural migrations that took place before the valleys were settled. But some mountains and valleys still lie hundreds of miles from any suburb, and elk still react to the coming of winter much as they did when Osborne Russell trapped beaver. If we know how elk react to snow, we still can find them during that early-winter period when the snow starts falling.

Light, early-season snowfalls often melt quickly, and the elk that went down the mountain often go back up. As autumn grows colder, the frost-cured grass of the mountain becomes more palatable again. Once it does, elk can tolerate fairly deep snow as long as it doesn't crust over, forcing them to use too much energy pawing through for a few bites of grass.

The days of the first snows in late fall or early winter are a time of transition for elk. Fall is trying to make up its mind at this time of year. On a morning a few days past the autumnal equinox, I'll get up and look out the window to see a perfectly level line on the side of the Elkhorn Mountains. Above that line the mountain is now white; below, the bare ridges are still brown, and the draws pale green or, sometimes, an almost too-bright yellow, filled by the dying leaves on quaking aspen.

Elk can move both downhill and uphill during winter, as changing weather creates better conditions either low or high.

119

By that afternoon, most of the snow will have melted from the conifers of the mountain, and in a few days most of the new snow will be gone again, except perhaps from the barren rock summit, above the timberline and the thaw line. Sometimes no more snow will fall until late October, or even November, but when it does, the level topographic line along the bottom of the snow will be lower than that of the September snow. This too may melt, or it may not, but eventually and inexorably this rising and falling snow-line creeps lower.

And so do the elk. Not only do they often move up and down the mountain as the snow level rises and falls, but they often travel just under the snow-line. Like most prey species, elk are very much aware that they leave tracks in snow. They also know that they are more visible against a white backdrop.

If enough snow falls, the ground just below snow-line will be soft enough to show the tracks of six or a dozen elk. Many hunters like to hunt 100 yards or so below the snow-line shortly after a storm, the sodden, shin-high brush of snowberries and ninebark quiet against their wool pants.

Mountain elk always like to bed on any level area. This is only natural, because if they fall asleep on steep hillsides they might roll off. During this transition period they especially like to bed along the edge of any ridge-end, facing downhill, where they can watch below for any predator, and where anything approaching from behind cannot see them through the tops of the trees on the ridge. This survival strategy is yet another reason many experienced early-season hunters like to travel sidehills, hoping to find elk bedded on one of these little "knobs" along any mountainside. Elk will have the advantage here, but if the ground is wet and quiet, they can often be smelled or even heard before they're seen. And a timber elk hunter should also squat or kneel down frequently, looking under the head-high branches of trees or brush. Elk on the ground can see your moving legs long before you'll see any part of them.

Keenly aware of hunting pressure, late-season elk often bed where they can see us coming. They also don't care for the first snows and often move just below the snow-line, where their tracks aren't as easily followed. This regressing old bull with a bad eye and non-typical rack could be facing his last winter.

Part Three

SPRING & SUMMER

FIRST GREEN

In spring ... elk move to calving grounds that offer some security to the widely distributed cows. Grizzly and black bears, wolves, wolverines and coyotes will try hard to locate the tasty newborns. Even eagles may strike elk calves, as one golden eagle did right in front of me on a day-old calf. He wheeled in to hit it four times and made it cry and stagger with each blow, but did not break the calf's skin. The aggressive raptor abandoned the calf when he saw me coming. The little elk then crouched and lay stiff as a board at my feet. A group of bighorn ewes came along and examined it cautiously. I departed too, in the hope that its mommy found the little elk.

Calves may bleat when in danger, and a cow elk readily rushes in to protect her calf against minor predators such as coyotes. These little wild dogs succeed only too well in the absence of the cow. Small calves drop into hiding upon the alarm bark of the cow elk; they come out of hiding or bleat in response to a high-pitched nasal whine uttered by the cow. When the calves grow larger, however, they will run to the cow during an alarm, ready to flee with her.

—*Valerius Geist*
Elk Country, *1991*

When the angle of the sun rises past the vernal equinox, the snow starts to disappear from the southern faces of ridges, especially in the valleys. Ice

---

Spring is a time of new growth for elk, both in bulls' antlers and cows' calves. Mature elk that survive the last snows of March have an excellent chance of seeing the next fall, but many young calves will die before then.

melts from the larger rivers, and though their waters will be "ice cold," their temperature still remains above freezing throughout the night, so the snow begins to melt along streambanks too. The snowmelt seeping into the thawing ground feeds early grasses and sedges, and the elk that have survived the winter converge on the green-up like ravens on an elk carcass. Elk come to eat the new grass and lick the minerals from the muddy earth, attempting to force nutrients into bodies that, over the last couple of months, have begun eating themselves, robbing muscles of protein to keep hearts pumping blood to brains.

Cow elk can appear anything but majestic at this time of year, their bellies big with unborn calves, their hips almost as bony as those of an old Jersey cow. The winter hair, so thick and sleek in September, but now bleached by the dry and cold sun of January, is matted like old hay. But the bulls, though thin, oddly enough still wear their huge antlers.

Calves are born around the time of spring's greening, allowing them to begin grazing on soft, nutritious food while their mothers recover from winter. This calf (right) has prospered well through spring and summer and has now grown a winter coat to match its mother's.

CASTING OLD ANTLERS

*T*his is one of the oddities of elk. Most other deer in North America—or indeed, temperate-zone deer from anywhere in the world—drop their antlers as soon as they aren't needed for the rut. Whether whitetails or mule deer, caribou or moose, they effectively become "female," living and eating in the same places as does and cows, often even in the same herd.

This antler-casting is triggered by the opposite effect of antler-hardening in late summer: a drop in "male" testosterone and a rise in "female" estrogen. Exactly when antlers fall off not only depends on the species, but the severity of the rut, the age and condition of the male, and that year's weather.

An Idaho friend once killed a big whitetail buck in early December, soon after the peak of the rut. When he grabbed an antler to drag the deer downhill, the antler came off in his hand. Young bucks often keep their spikes or forks long into winter, but

Elk retain their antlers longer than any other North American deer. Many winter ranges are covered with shed antlers in May.

the latest I've seen antlers on a mature northern deer, either whitetail or mule deer, was in early February of a very mild winter as a friend and I drove through the Missouri Breaks to visit a rancher we knew. As our pickup came around a bend on a winding gravel road, we saw a medium-sized mule deer buck feeding on the next hillside, antlers bleached white and obviously ready to fall off. Both moose and caribou bulls lose their antlers a month or two after the early-fall rut.

But it's common to see March bachelor herds of bull elk still wearing their six-point antlers. The latest I've personally seen mature elk with antlers was in mid-April, just about income tax day, on a visit to the National Bison Range. Eileen and I were driving along Mission Creek, looking at the first mallards of spring, when two really big bull elk stood up in the alders right next to the creek. I took two photographs before they turned to leave, their backs still broad and massive, brown antlers still firmly

Mature bull elk often exit winter while still in their bachelor bands. Some bulls even retain their antlers into April.

attached—or at least they seemed to be, since the bulls trotted off through the thick willows and young cottonwood trees along the creek, where loose antlers would have readily been knocked off.

Why do bull elk keep their antlers so long? As noted above, males of the other deer of North America tend to live with or near the females over the winter, at a time when the females need all the food they can get, to feed their unborn fawns and calves. If bulls retained their antlers, they'd also retain a higher rank than the females, and consequently eat more of the best food. Caribou cows are the only North American female deer that also grow antlers in order to compete for food with young bulls on their wintering grounds, at a time of year when most mature bulls have already lost their antlers—and rank. Whitetails, mule deer and moose are all much less herd-oriented than caribou or elk, so few conflicts arise, and the males can lose their antlers and rank without nutritional consequences.

But aside from the rut, mature bull elk live in their bachelor groups, away from the herds of cows, calves and immature bulls. There are exceptions, such as the feeding grounds in Jackson Hole, but by and large, mature bulls stay away from the cow herds, and retain their antlers to keep the question of rank settled over the winter. This pecking order was decided back in late summer and early fall, during the sparring matches of early September and the real conflicts of the rut. But that was a time of abundant green food, and when rank really mattered: He who gathered the most cows won.

In winter, even sparring matches could drain enough energy to leave a

After a bull's antlers drop, his pedicles remain raw for a few days. But changes in hormone levels quickly stimulate new antler growth.

bull susceptible to disease or predators or both. So bull elk retain their antlers throughout the winter—longer, in fact, than any other north-country deer. Red deer evolved in slightly warmer climates; winters in much of Europe are normally warmed by occasional winds from the oceans, unlike the cold "continental" winters of much of North America. So red deer cast their antlers earlier than elk, when the earlier spring of Europe reduces conflicts over food.

But spring comes much later in the heart of North American elk habitat. On the winter ranges surrounding Yellowstone and many other valleys in the Rocky Mountains, true spring doesn't begin until April in most years. So the elk retain their antlers until then—and start growing new ones almost as soon as the old ones fall. If you hang around elk for many springs, you'll often see a bull, with bloody pedicles, that obviously just lost his antlers. A week later the same bull may show the stumps of his new antlers, growing like lumpy mushrooms between his ears.

The timing of the elk rut is, to a certain extent, genetically programmed from the tens of thousands of years that elk evolved in northern Asia.

Tule Calving Time: Still Evolving

Our elk are so recent to the continent that they still retain the late-September/early-October rut, which brings calves into the world in the days surrounding June 1st, when spring grass and forbs can provide food for both the cow and calf.

But elk are still evolving in North America.

Spring green-up in California is a more extended process, beginning earlier than in the mountains of Siberia or the Rockies, and after a milder winter. While on one hand, calves being born within a two-week period helps to "flood" the herd with new calves so that predators can't eat all of them at once, overall calf survival can also be helped if some are born outside the main calving time.

These out-of-norm young receive even less attention from predators keying on prime-time young, and with abundant food available there's no disadvantage for some cow elk to have early or late calves. (This is the reason that most tropical deer have no seasonal breeding season—or a very long one, taking place over several months. With food and cover growing all year, there's no advantage to a concentrated birth season. We also see something of this drawn-out rut in southern whitetails, which may rut over a couple of months, rather than the sharp two- to three-week rut of northern deer.)

So deer that evolve in cold-weather climates often develop a longer rut when living in warmer climates. This is caused by early and late young passing on their own mother's tendency to come into estrus outside the "normal" peak. In California, the earlier spring has allowed early Tule elk calves to survive for millennia, with the result that many females come into estrus in August, and some even in July, before the bulls have shed their velvet. So the usual structure of the rut—with males very ready to mate and the first estrus females becoming the "rut detonator"—is somewhat reversed. Some early-estrus females "force" the bulls to start bugling and mating in summer, and Tule elk keep evolving to fit their unusual elk environment.

IN WITH  NEW ANTLERS

Over the next three to four months a mature bull elk will regrow a pair of antlers 4 feet long. In the heat of summer, the antlers often can grow more than an inch per day. This seems to be an amazing amount, but in reality elk have smaller antlers for their body size than many other deer. A caribou bull, for example, weighs half as much as an elk bull, yet he will grow antlers about as long and large as that of a bull elk. It is interesting that, despite the size of caribou antlers,

A mature bull's antlers begin to grow almost as soon as his old ones fall off, usually before he sheds his winter hair. The new bumps are extremely tender, one reason late spring bulls prefer open country.

they are much lighter in weight than elk antlers of similar size. I have a set of big caribou antlers from Canada's Northwest Territories that, with the complete skull, weighs less than nine pounds; a six-point bull elk's rack of similar size will weigh twice as much.

The weight difference probably occurs because of body size. A deer's antlers are bone, primarily made of calcium and phosphorus. No deer can eat enough mineral-rich food over a short summer season to grow large antlers, so the minerals are drawn from

the deer's own skeleton. Consequently, the other bones of male deer actually suffer seasonally from osteoporosis—bone-weakening through loss of calcium—though when the antlers reach full growth and harden, their skeletons quickly recover.

Caribou are the prototypical open-country deer of the north, so bulls "need" large antlers to display to caribou cows that might be watching from a long distance. Relative to body size, caribou grow the largest antlers of any deer, often with palmated tops, the better to show up across a tundra valley, especially when a bull (like all male deer in rut) lifts his head to show off his long-beamed crown.

The largest-bodied caribou grow along the 60th parallel of latitude—a line running through southern Alaska, then along the northern boundary of British Columbia, Alberta and Manitoba, and across northern Quebec. A big bull may weigh more than 500 pounds, especially in the mountains of western

Elk grow antlers about the size of caribou antlers. But elk are much larger-bodied than caribou (right); relative to their body size, elk antlers are smaller, a result of their mixed-country environment.

Canada. This is a large mammal, but still only half the size of a big bull elk. Northern bull caribou, from the Arctic Slope of Alaska or the tundra along the Arctic Ocean in Canada, are noticeably smaller, often no larger than a big mule deer. But they still grow huge antlers rivaling those of bull elk—but in size, not in weight. Because caribou are smaller than elk, they cannot afford to draw as many minerals from their own skeleton, and so caribou antlers are more "full of air" than elk antlers.

Elk antlers do not rival moose antlers, neither in weight of antlers nor in relationship to body weight. A big Alaska moose can be twice the size of the average mature elk, weigh-

ing well more than 1,500 pounds, and sometimes grows antlers weighing three times as much as an elk's. I have a set from an average mature Alaskan bull, representative but not exceptional in either width or mass, that weighs 43 pounds complete with skull. A really large Alaska moose rack will weigh 60 pounds or more.

The difference here occurs because moose live and feed much of the year in lush riparian habitat. Willows, that favorite moose food, are particularly high in calcium and phosphorus. Elk feed much of the year on mineral-deficient grasses and sedges. So despite the grandeur of a big elk's rack, they really aren't the antler champions of the deer world.

TO BUILD AN ANTLER

It takes a lot of blood to carry calcium and other bone-building minerals to an elk's antlers, and to feed the oily, short-haired skin we call "velvet." Some good-sized blood vessels lie between the building bone and the skin of the velvet. The vessels fit into grooves on the surface of the growing bone, plainly visible on clean, hard antlers, like the imprints of prehistoric mollusks in sea-bottom shale. If you stand close enough to a bull elk in late summer, you can sometimes even see the pulse of arteries under the brick-red velvet.

While the antlers are growing and not yet hard, they feel almost rubbery, like cartilage. So much blood pumps through the rapidly-growing tissue that living antlers can be even warmer than a bull's body.

One theory about the evolutionary reason for antlers suggests that midsummer antlers also act as radiators, helping to cool elk (and other deer, especially moose) during hot weather. Bachelor bands of velvet-clad bulls do tend to hang out in the open more during summer, rather than risk bumping their soft antlers against hard trees, so perhaps they need the extra cooling effect of multi-tined heat-exchangers on their heads.

If a bull elk injures his antlers during growth, some sort of deformity may result. I've seen several elk racks with one perfectly-formed antler, the other a heavy down-dropping blob with a few short tines. Observations of captive elk suggest these "hammer horns" probably result from a heavy blow to the pedicle during early growth. In later stages of antler development, the soft bone often breaks instead of growing in odd ways. One year in Montana on opening day of bow season, I killed a "five-point" bull that had broken his right antler off above the bez tine a few weeks before. The velvet had grown over the break, rounding off the stub of the main beam, but otherwise the broken antler hardened normally.

Like other deer, elk injured in the leg or body often grow a malformed antler on the opposite side. A broken right hind leg, for instance, often causes the left antler to grow weirdly.

Bull moose grow the largest antlers of any of the world's deer. Moose live in more nutrient-rich riparian habitat than elk or caribou, allowing the luxury of growing antlers that often weigh 60 pounds or more.

Often, such antlers are smaller and tend to droop, perhaps because they normally draw calcium from a particular part of the skeleton during growth. The injury allows fewer minerals to reach the antler.

While the vast majority of bull elk grow typical 6x6 antlers from age three onward, a few elk do grow odd points on their antlers, the result of some blip in their DNA.

One bull who lived on the National Bison Range developed an extra tine at the base of each brow tine. I was one of many photographers who took Kodachromes of him every season. During his second antler year, when most bulls grow 5x5 racks, those extra, upright tines that were first visible as short spikes continued to grow throughout his life until a poacher shot him and cut off his head one day soon after his antlers had hardened. The rack never did surface, probably because it was too distinctive. One fall a massive bull appeared in Mammoth with a huge 9x10 rack that made the normally impressive "royal" racks of the other rutting bulls appear rather puny.

Antlers in general, especially those in velvet, have long been used as medication in much of Asia, particularly China. Typically, dried velvet antler is sliced into thin wafers, but sometimes the velvet alone is ground up. Either eaten or brewed into tea, "live" antler (as opposed to antlers without velvet) is supposedly good for a variety of ailments, but most commonly "prescribed" as a cure for human male impotence. A few men I know have tried it, with varied results.

But the idea makes sense, since some forms of impotence are the result of a drop in testosterone level as we age. Antler-hardening is a direct result of rising testosterone levels, so testosterone should occur in the antlers, especially during the last week or so before the bone fully hardens. For a number of years, elk "ranchers" made a lot of money cutting almost-grown antlers from their bulls and selling them to Asian brokers, but I understand that Viagra knocked some of the starch out of the velvet market. Some Western medicines are evidently more effective than traditional Chinese remedies.

Bull elk typically grow six tines on each antler at maturity, but occasional extreme variations on the theme occur. They aren't common, however, because bulls with irregular antlers usually don't breed with as many cows as bulls with "typical" headgear, so they don't pass on their irregular traits.

NON-TYPICAL ELK

For decades the Boone and Crockett Club's book, *Records of North American Big Game*, only accepted elk racks that scored "typically," meaning that any tines considered abnormal (more than seven to an antler) counted *against* the total score. But some hunters had taken huge elk racks over the decades, heads that were obviously larger than many "book" entries, and started pressuring B & C for another category for "non-typical" antlers, such as those listed in several deer categories.

Eventually, B & C complied, and beginning with the 1993 edition of the records book, a new non-typical American elk category was included.

B & C does not differentiate between Manitoba and Rocky Mountain elk in this category, and the initial world record came from Manitoba, taken north of Riding Mountain National Park back in 1961 by James R. Berry, who over the years kept the rack more as an impressive curiosity than anything else. He remembers that the bull weighed more than 1,200 pounds, and that he killed it with one shot from his .30-30 Win. It has eight tines on one antler, nine on the other, weighs 38 pounds and scored 447$\frac{1}{8}$ points.

COMING OUT PARTY

By early August the antlers are almost grown and only the very tips are still rubbery. Around the middle of the month the velvet begins to die, and the bulls begin "polishing" their hard bone on brush and young trees.

There's some debate about whether this brush-thrashing is the result of a desire to get rid of dead velvet, and how much is due to "testosterone rage." In theory, the antlers are dead by the time the velvet comes off, so the bulls can't feel it itching or peeling. Sometimes long strips do hang down in their faces, which must be annoying. But no matter why they get rid of it so rapidly, it's amazing to see bulls in velvet one week, and

all but the spikes and a few raghorns peeled down and ready to fight the next.

Freshly peeled antlers tend to be pink: new white bone with a faint wash of blood. But within a few days the bone turns darker. Some people claim the brownish color is a result of the blood clotting and drying, others say it comes from the bark and sap of the brush and trees pre-rut bull elk attack. Probably it's a combination of both. I do know that elk (and deer) from areas near fire-burns tend to have darker antlers, probably from charred bark. And elk from truly open country like the Missouri Breaks or, especially, California's central valley, often have

When antlers harden in late August, their velvet skin peels rather quickly. Bulls help the process by rubbing their antlers on any nearby object, especially small conifers.

paler antlers than those of timber elk, especially if there aren't many conifer trees around, which have stickier sap than that of deciduous trees or brush.

It's indisputable that the tips of a bull elk's tines, the part of the antler that's polished when he feeds in long grass, or digs up the earth near a wallow, remain a shining ivory even when the beams of his antlers are almost black. In fact, that's often how you'll first find a bull elk in the deep shadows of "black" timber: through the symmetrical line of white tines, like candles along a chandelier. Sometimes they seem to shine almost as brightly.

Just what is a "royal" bull elk? These days, most American hunters tend to refer to elk antlers by the number of tines on each antler: 5-point, 6-point or, sometimes, referring to both antlers, as in 5x5 or 6x7. Any bull with fewer than five points is generally considered a "raghorn" or occasionally a "brush horn," and young bulls with simple beams are called "spikes," even if one or both of their antlers fork (as they sometimes do) at the top. Serious trophy hunters often refer to the antler "score" as tabulated by the Boone and Crockett Club, a long-time conservation organization. Some even combine the two methods, for instance saying "the bull was a big 6x6, around 340 or 350 B & C."

But some hunters still refer to mature bull elk as "royal" bulls. What the term means, and where it came from, is an interesting story and yet really doesn't resolve the occasional argument about whether a royal bull has six or seven points on each antler.

A bull elk will typically grow spikes during his second year, five-tined antlers in his third year, six tines in his fourth year, and sometimes seven or more tines on each antler after that, though six is the usual number.

Each tine normally grows directly out of the main beam of the antler, so the antler must grow longer to add succeeding points.

The term "royal" originated in the British Isles in reference to red deer antlers. Red deer also usually grow five tines on each antler during their third year, but in succeeding years, the fifth tine often forks, or splits into three or more tines, forming a "crown" at the tip. (Other Europeans also recognize the same crown, Germans call it the *Krone*, French the *empaumure ou coronne*.) British and European royalty wore crowns, so a red deer stag with a crown became known as a royal. In English terminology, royal antlers have seven tines, four along the beam and the 3-tined crown at the end of the beam.

But crowning is very uncommon among American elk antlers. It happens most frequently in coastal Roosevelt elk and occasionally in Tule elk, but crowning is very rare in Rocky Mountain and Manitoba bulls. Which is why there's still some argument over what constitutes "royal" elk antlers. A mature North American bull elk normally grows six tines on each antler throughout his life, and so is considered the equivalent of a mature red deer: a royal.

But some hunters insist that only the more unusual 7-point antlers deserve the special appellation "royal," despite not forming any sort of a crown. Other hunters supposedly call 7x7 bulls imperials, and 8x8s monarchs. At least that's what the occasional reference book states.

I have lived in Montana most of my life, with a year each in Idaho and Wyoming, as well as a summer and fall in the western Canadian province of Alberta, and I have never heard anybody in any of those places call a bull elk an imperial or a monarch. (Other reference books sometimes refer to "gray partridge" and "trombone-action" shotguns as alternatives to Hungarian and pumpgun. Again, I have never heard anybody use either gray or trombone when referring to partridge or shotguns, which leads to the suspicion that some reference books simply copy older reference books.)

Today, the tines of North American elk antlers are commonly referred to as the brow (the first over the eye), the bez or bay (second tine up), the trez or trey (third tine), and the dagger (the typically long fourth tine); thereafter tines are simply referred to by their number: 5th, 6th, 7th, and so on. You will occasionally hear somebody referring to the last point on a big bull's antler as the royal tine, regardless of whether it's the 6th, 7th or 8th—at which point you may begin a heated discussion, or simply choose to nod agreeably.

REPLENISHING ✦ HERD

While the bulls grow their antlers, the cows raise their calves. Which is more important?

It's natural, perhaps even instinctive, to defend motherhood in all its natural, mythical and even religious significance. But the scientific fact is that the antler growth of a big bull weakens his body about as much as a growing fetus drains a cow. And in the long evolutionary run, the genetic choosing of big-antlered, "successful" males may be as important as calf-birth.

But after the cows become pregnant, the bulls are expendable. Or at least most of them are, which is why so few bulls survive in the wild, even in unhunted populations. Now it's up to the pregnant cows to produce the next generation.

During winter, cows tend to band together in large herds, mostly for protection from predators: the "selfish herd" protecting most of its members through the rules of chance. More pairs of eyes tend to see more wolves and mountain lions, and more elk

New calves average only about 20 pounds at birth but can follow their mothers easily within a week.

CONSERVATION ORGANIZATIONS

The problem of decreasing winter range has been recognized for more than a century by hunters and other conservationists. Many today have realized that the only sure way that significant winter range can be saved from development is by buying it or by making conservation grants to landowners that keep the land from ever being "developed." Among these are the Mule Deer Foundation, the Foundation for North American Wild Sheep, the North American Pronghorn Foundation and, above all, that quintessential elk organization, the Rocky Mountain Elk Foundation. All of these also fund essential wildlife research, as do two major hunting organizations: the Boone and Crockett Club and the Pope and Young Club. Anybody concerned about the future of wildlife should join one or more of these organizations.

Rocky Mountain Elk Foundation
2291 West Broadway
P.O. Box 8249
Missoula, MT 59807
(800) 225-5355
www.rmef.org

Mule Deer Foundation
1005 Terminal Way, Suite 170
Reno, NV 89502
(775) 322-6558
www.muledeer.org

Foundation for North
American Wild Sheep
720 Allen Avenue
Cody, WY 82414
(307) 527-6261
www.fnaws.org

North American Pronghorn
Foundation
1905 CY Avenue
Casper, WY 82604
(307) 235-6273
www.antelope.org

Boone and Crockett Club
Old Milwaukee Depot
250 Station Drive
Missoula, MT 59801
(406) 542-1888
www.boone-crockett.org

Pope and Young Club
P.O. Box 548
Chatfield, MN 55923
(507) 867-4144
www.pope-young.org

Safari Club International
4800 West Gates Pass Road
Tucson, AZ 85745
(520) 620-1220
www.safariclub.org

means any individual cow is less likely to be eaten.

More mature elk are killed by "natural" predators during winter than at any other time of year. Snow makes it difficult for heavy, hooved animals to run away, but only lightly hinders soft-pawed wolves and mountain lions. And the elk are weakened, especially as winter gets old but still hangs on, by lack of high-calorie food and by extended cold. So carnivores often fatten during snowy winters, while elk die.

The selfish herds continue to hold together during early spring, the green-up weeks of April and early May. By the first of April, the unborn calves are almost fully formed, but the early green growth plays a large part in calf survival.

Studies have shown that a higher protein content in a cow's diet over the last half of its pregnancy results in a larger calf. Depending on the maturity of the mother—bigger cows have bigger calves—and on her diet during late pregnancy, calves may weigh anywhere from 20 to 45 pounds at birth. One study showed that newborn calves weighing more than 35 pounds stood a 90 percent chance of living through the next month (the stage of life when most elk mortality takes place), while calves with a birth weight of 25 pounds or less had, at most, a 50 percent chance for survival.

Elk have evolved in several ways to overcome the vulnerability of newborn calves. As mentioned, the rut's timing ensures that most births will be almost coincident. After a typical

Most winter-killed elk die from disease and predators, not starvation. This carcass is surrounded by wolf tracks, but did the wolves kill the elk or only scavenge what was already dead?

YELLOWSTONE POACHING

Yellowstone Park was established by an act of Congress in 1872, which included a clause prohibiting the "wanton destruction of the fish and game within said park." But no money was set aside to enforce that clause. The 1870s and early 1880s were perhaps the darkest era of wildlife destruction in North America. Hide hunters killed off the buffalo with the explicit blessing of the United States Army, in order to starve the Plains tribes and move them onto reservations. Market hunters killed wildfowl and big game by the tens of thousands, but before refrigerated railroad cars, most of the meat didn't make it to market. Everywhere in the United States, wild game was disappearing, which many folks thought inevitable, a means of clearing the land for "civilization."

One of the fast-disappearing big game animals was the elk. Not only did they provide a lot of meat and durable, supple leather, but their ivory "tusks" were in demand, especially by members of the Benevolent and Protective Order of Elks. Even before the establishment of Yellowstone Park, western wildlife was being wiped out. Several expeditions exploring the country just before and after 1872 could not support themselves by hunting, because there was practically no game—in the same area that trapper Osborne Russell wrote of as a game paradise in the 1830s.

But in the years after its making, Yellowstone Park, on the highest plateau in the center of the northern Rocky Mountains, became the last refuge for many mobile big game animals, especially bison and elk. And so the market hunters went there, even after 1872. One of the first private concessionaires, the so-called Park Improvement Company, even fed workers on game killed in the park. In 1882, the Park Improvement Company contracted with market hunters for 10 tons of wild meat. Eventually there was a public outcry, and in 1886 the U.S. Cavalry was sent to protect the park. They essentially ran Yellowstone until 1916, when the National Park Service was created.

For the most part, the soldiers did a good job. Mounted soldiers easily kept poachers out of the park during summer, so tusk hunters eventually killed in winter instead, snowshoeing or cross-country skiing up to elk helpless in deep snow. So the U.S. Cavalry, the "horse soldiers" of the Indian Wars, also learned to snowshoe and ski, and eventually convinced poachers to stay away from Yellowstone. By 1890, the elk had increased to several thousand, and by 1912, the year the first elk census was made, the official number was 30,101.

But a few elk are still poached every year. Not all that long ago, a Georgia poacher with a bow, Don Lewis, was convicted of killing elk in Yellowstone. Lewis, who had been hired as a professional hunter by several bowhunting equipment firms, evidently felt pressure to produce big elk every year, and made several annual trips to Yellowstone, videoing the "hunts" he and companions made inside the park. Eventually, he was caught by Utah authorities who were investigating reports of deer poaching; when they searched Lewis's pickup truck they found the videos, which were recognized as being made in Yellowstone. So elk poaching in our greatest national park did not end when the U.S. Cavalry rode in more than a century ago, and it will continue as long as humans can make money by illegally killing wild game.

late-September through early-October breeding season, most calves will be born in the last part of May or in early June. In most years, this coincides with the first truly lush growth of spring greenery, so the mother elk will have plenty of quality food to help her produce milk high in protein.

This high-protein milk—and lots of it—is absolutely necessary for the survival of the calf during its first few weeks of life. Milk doesn't nourish the calf as well as the direct shot of protein it got through the umbilical cord, so more volume is needed to cover the difference. The cow needs to eat even better when the calf is suckling (no more dry twigs, Mom!) than when the calf was developing in her womb. This is why most calving occurs during peak green-up.

This scenario of birthing calves during peak spring green-up is due not to wise planning by elk subcommittees,

Newborn elk calves require high-protein milk. If they don't get it, they will grow slowly and are in danger of not surviving the next winter.

but to genetics. Over thousands of generations, the elk calves born before and after spring green-up tended not to survive as well. Calves born too early either froze to death, or their mothers didn't get enough high-protein food to produce good milk—or enough of it—and the weakened calves either froze or were eaten. Calves born too late also tended to be eaten because they couldn't keep up with the selfish herd—or because they went into winter underweight and thus were vulnerable to cold, snow and the predators they managed to escape in summer.

HOW CALVES SURVIVE

Elk are large animals, designed by thousands of generations of open-country flight from wolves to be able to run both fast and far. But it takes an average calf two or three weeks to develop its running gear. The sooner it can run, the more likely it will survive.

Some other large prey animals fight hard and effectively against wolves and other large carnivores. A cow moose can often drive off a pack of wolves with her hooves. Bison and musk oxen band together, males and females, to guard their newborn calves. But cow elk seem singularly helpless against large predators, despite their willingness to slash out with their front hooves against other elk.

So a new, unsteady calf's best bet for survival lies in hiding. Young calves are very good at instantly flopping to the ground, almost squirming into the earth and surrounding vegetation, and lying absolutely still. The newborn young of deer and pronghorns survive this way too. Even though elk are very large, they've retained this characteristic from their smaller red deer ancestors.

The cow enhances her calf's hideout flop by leaving the herd just before giving birth. Until calving

The birth of an elk calf usually coincides with the first green growth of spring, which provides the maximum amount of nutrition to the calf's mother and, hence, its mother's milk.

season, the selfish herd has helped elk survival, but since young calves can't run from predators, they would be more easily found and eaten. Large herds always attract predators, so near-birth cows drift away from the main herd. A lone cow isn't nearly as conspicuous as a dozen or more, and is less likely to be spotted by wolves, coyotes or mountain lions.

Roosevelt elk live in more heavily timbered country than do Rocky Mountain, Manitoba or Tule elk. They've adapted in several ways to thick cover: the bulls grow shorter antlers—the better to slide between trees—and the cows look for even thicker cover to give birth. Rocky Mountain and Tule cows, on the other hand, tend to give birth in fairly open country, often at the "edge" between meadows and timber.

I see cows with new calves in areas where I never see elk any other time of year. One place lies a mile up an old logging road, in an area where several draws full of quaking aspens come together at the head of a tiny stream. It's great ruffed grouse habitat, so I head up there several times

An elk calf spends much of its early life hiding while its mother feeds—and the mothers themselves often split off from the rest of the herd before giving birth. Both behaviors minimize predation.

a year to photograph or hunt the birds. But I almost never see elk except in May and June, when the odd cow hides in the aspens to give birth, leaving her other cow-buddies higher on the mountain.

Aspens and calves often go together: aspens need a lot of water, so typically grow near springs, which also feed the new grass of spring. A cow has everything she needs right there: food, water and places for her calf to hide from weather and predators.

Several years ago, I was hunting black bears in late May with my friends Melvin and John Forbes of West Virginia. We were working our way down a little creek-bottom, checking the patches of green grass along its riparian flats for a grazing bear.

We found no bears, but halfway down we startled a cow elk. She didn't follow the creek's cover, as she would likely do in fall, but ran up a sagebrush hillside and stood there, looking

While most elk give birth to one calf, occasionally twins are born. Cow elk tend to live in certain calving areas in spring, typically near spring seeps, which provide abundant water and green feed for milk production.

at us. From the sage at her feet, her new calf rose on unsteady legs and stood under her chest, wobbling, while she watched us carefully. We moved slowly off, not wanting to tire the new elk any more than

necessary. She'd evidently left the calf lying in knee-high sagebrush while she fed in the lusher grass along the creek—a good idea on her part, because black bears eat not only spring grass but young elk.

WHAT EATS ELK

One Idaho elk study was commissioned in the 1970s because the traditionally abundant elk along the Lochsa-Clearwater drainage were disappearing. The drop wasn't due to overhunting, since the human take had fallen steadily in recent years. Lo and behold, the researchers found that black bears were killing and eating more than half the elk calves in the study area.

Wolves also eat elk calves. (So what else is new?) When wolves were reintroduced to Yellowstone Park, after being killed off in the early part of the 20th century, they almost immediately started eating elk calves. How many, nobody knows; elk calves are very good at hiding, and provide only one small meal to the average seven-member wolf pack. Elk calves disappear quickly into wolf stomachs, as opposed to mature elk, which often try to escape by running across open country, and then provide at least two days of food to a pack.

From their studies, Park biologists estimate wolves kill about 500 mature elk a year. But the only real indication of calf-kill comes when the elk migrate to winter ranges several months later. There, elk can easily be counted, and the number of calves per cow can be observed. One spring there were only seven calves per 100 cows, by far the lowest cow-calf ratio observed in decades. Not all of those missing calves were eaten by wolves, of course, but it's probable that most were.

This drop in "recruitment" (as wildlife biologists call the addition of new calves to the herd) has caused some Montana hunters to predict the death of the Yellowstone elk herd, which they hunt each fall and winter as elk migrate out of the park. I think we should wait and see what evolves. Not so long ago, Yellowstone's elk hadn't even smelled a wild wolf in three-quarters of a century, and were pretty naive. Plus there were too damn many elk in the first place.

Over the years I've noticed that the average hunter never thinks there's

Wolves have recently reappeared in the American Rockies, as the result of both transplants and natural drift down from Canada. Wolves are perhaps the most efficient big game predators in North America; their long-term impact on elk numbers remains to be seen.

enough of any kind of game unless he sees elk (or deer, or pheasants) all the time. If an elk hunter from Livingston, Montana, isn't seeing elk while driving south on Highway 89 toward Mammoth, Wyoming, at the entrance of the park, he thinks they've all been gobbled by wolves.

But Monte Schnur, a hunting outfitter who lives "up the crick" from me, specializes in bighorn sheep and elk in the high country just north of Yellowstone. Monte has seen some

interesting things since the wolves came back.

Like many hunters, Monte didn't think much of the idea of wolf reintroduction before it occurred. But in the few years since, he's been rethinking his position. For one thing, he's seeing far more bighorn sheep lambs and mountain goat kids than he used to, and suspects the reason is that wolves kill coyotes. They have, in fact, killed many of the Park coyotes. About the only survivors are the

Coyotes normally eat smaller game—voles or deer fawns—but given the opportunity, they will take a calf elk, especially injured or weakened calves like this one.

The average hunter might be called semiskilled. Most wild mammals are by nature secretive, especially during hunting seasons, and many hunters simply don't know how to find them.

A few years ago, the Montana Department of Fish, Wildlife and Parks (FWP) interviewed mule deer hunters in the Missouri Breaks over several seasons, then compared hunters' perceptions of deer populations vs. the actual counts made by FWP biologists. Most hunters felt there were good numbers of deer in years when there were five or more mule deer per square mile, but if average deer numbers dropped to four per square mile—a mere 20 percent drop—many hunters complained about low populations.

Why? Eventually the biologists (most of them avid mule deer hunters) sorted it out. Only when mule deer are actually a little too abundant do some deer start living in more open and accessible country—especially mature bucks. In "average" years, the larger

bucks tend to live in deeper canyons, often in and around juniper thickets, and away from roads—exactly the sorts of places avoided by average hunters, most of whom would like to kill a "good" buck but are really leaving that up to chance. So if they don't see mule deer bucks in the easily accessible country they normally hunt, they perceive mule deer populations as low.

Elk hunters aren't much different. Many don't have the skill to track elk into thicker cover, and most don't want to pack elk quarters out of steep canyons, so they avoid those places. Elk soon realize this and start living in "black timber" in deep drainages, and the average hunter starts complaining about a lack of elk.

When elk populations really started to rise in the 1960s, and some herds began attacking winter haystacks because they'd outgrown their winter range, another Montana survey showed that

the average elk hunter simply didn't believe that there could

Now You See Them, Now You Don't

be too many elk. Why? Because Montana elk hunters really knew their stuff. Elk could never outgrow their habitat, because the state's skilled hunters would always keep them in check. Today, elk numbers are still growing all over the West. Where are those really good elk hunters?

coyotes living near the few highways in Yellowstone, since wolves tend to avoid highways.

Plus, Monte's noticed, the wolves tend to stay down in the valleys, away from bighorns and mountain goats and the big bull elk that like to live in the high country. He's also seeing more big bulls up near timberline since the wolves moved in, though that may also be due to the dry winters of late. In dry years, the greenest grass grows high on the mountains.

So I am willing to wait and see, and not start howling "wolf" before everything shakes out. Wolves may even help the Park, though probably not by "controlling" the overabundant bison, as was the hope of many wolf enthusiasts. The Yellowstone wolves have shown a marked aversion toward eating buffalo, probably because adult buffalo can defend themselves, and are very good at "circling up" to defend their calves. Hunting down and eating a bison calf is just too much work … and too dangerous.

MOOSE IN THE MINORITY

I grew up 90 miles from Yellowstone and have visited it virtually every summer or fall of my life. When I was a kid in the 1950s and '60s, both buffalo and elk were fairly uncommon in the Park. Oh, we'd see some every trip, but each sighting was an event. Lately elk are everywhere, and buffalo almost so. But I almost never see the other large mammals I saw during family trips when I was a kid: mule deer, the occasional white-tailed deer, bighorn sheep and, especially, moose.

In my father's collection of home movies, there's one scene taken in September, sometime in the early 1960s, during the moose rut. On the edge of a marsh, nine mature bull moose are hovering around one poor cow, bluff-charging each other and pleading for her attention.

In all the years since, I may have seen a total of nine bull moose in

---

Elk are big animals that require a lot of water, and they tend to spend time near streams whenever they can. Along with bison, their stream-visiting has had a large effect on streambank vegetation in Yellowstone Park, harming moose habitat.

Yellowstone Park, and I've spent some time looking for them, in all the best remaining habitat. Why so few moose? Too many elk and, to some extent, buffalo. They've eaten and beaten down the willow cover along most creeks and rivers so much that moose don't have anywhere to live. Of course, wolves are very fond of moose meat too, and seem to have made a considerable dent in the few remaining Yellowstone moose. But give the wolves a few years among the elk, and the willows may grow up again into fine moose habitat. If the moose have enough willows to hide in, some will survive the wolves.

The state of Wyoming has long fed wintering elk in the Jackson Hole area. Whether this large gathering of wintering elk is good for the herd—or the local ecosystem—has been controversial.

PROBLEM ELK

*T*he whole question here comes down to the popular catch-word "biodiversity." What has occurred with Yellowstone's elk over the past few decades is starting to happen with elk herds elsewhere. Elk are magnificent animals, but are hundreds of thousands of elk worth diminishing the rest of the wildlife of the West? That's why I'm willing to wait, along with Monte Schnur, to see the eventual result of the Yellowstone wolves on the Yellowstone elk.

There's some evidence that elk also out-compete mule deer on winter range. Elk are bigger, so they can eat almost anything and digest enough to

survive. Mule deer (and whitetails) are rather delicate eaters in comparison, requiring specialized winter food. So if elk overrun winter range, deer tend to suffer.

One Idaho study showed the same relationship between elk, mule deer and roads as the relationship between Yellowstone wolves, coyotes and roads. Most of the mule deer in the study area were found near roads—from blacktop highways to one-lane logging roads—while elk were found "over the hill" in the backcountry, as has been shown in other places. The study's biologists hypothesize that since mule deer can tolerate vehicles and elk can't, increasingly abundant elk in the backcountry are "pushing" the deer toward areas with fewer elk, either through sheer numbers or through actual competition for food. (Unlike politicians, biologists almost always "hypothesize," which means they make an educated guess about what's happening, rather than make a firm statement about anything, because they work in a world full of thousands of variables. Of course politicians do too, but they would like us to think they have The Simple Answer to every complex problem. Which is the problem with politicians managing wildlife.)

THE HEIGHT OF SUMMER

Of elk calves taken by predators, most are younger than one month old. After that age, the youngsters can usually keep up with their mothers, so the cows start drifting back together into selfish herds. Often the cows feed in the open at this time of year, which provides a certain measure of security once the calves can keep up. It's hard for a mountain lion to sneak up on a herd of elk in a wide meadow.

Plus, more open country may be relatively free of biting insects like mosquitoes, horseflies and deerflies. At this time of year, late June through September, certain elevations of the Rocky Mountains

Late-summer elk often feed in the open—to eat the rich grass and to avoid insects.

resemble the tundra of the Far North. In fact, some parts are tundra, evidence of the old scientific rule that both altitude and latitude affect ecozones. Tundra is open ground that lies frozen except during a brief summer, when it turns into grassy ridges and swampy bottoms. In a particularly wet year even the ridges can resemble long green sponges. I have hiked lots of tundra, both in the subarctic regions of Canada and Alaska and high in the Rockies during July and August, finding springs welling from the ground almost on top of some ridges.

Lots of clean, standing water is what breeds mosquitoes and many other "biting" insects, so elk often frequent breezy ridges at this time of year, allowing the wind to blow the bugs away. I've seen herds of 50 or more cows and calves, brick-red in their summer coats, lying scattered across kelly-green ridges in the middle of a mountain basin in late June. Higher in the basin, along the edge of

A few days after giving birth, elk mothers tend to drift back together, forming nursery herds. One cow will often accompany several calves, allowing the other mothers to graze uninterrupted for a little while.

Summer elk can often be found on open ridges, where breezes blow away biting insects. The spring snowmelt leaves pools of pure water, perfect breeding grounds for mosquitoes.

Elk "molt" in spring, ridding themselves of the thick undercoat that provides insulation throughout winter. Bulls molt first, primarily because they're bigger, and their sheer size means their bodies retain more heat, even without a winter coat.

The long "guard hair," which provides most of the elk's visible color, is much like deer hair—hollow and fairly light; the woolly winter undercoat provides the most important insulation against cold. The undercoat develops over the fall, and takes a lot of energy to produce, so the bulls that use the least energy during the rut are best protected against a long winter. A well-developed winter pelt has such a high "R-factor" that healthy bulls with a thick undercoat often wear a mantle of new-fallen snowflakes: Their undercoat doesn't even allow their body heat to melt snow.

The molt begins when the thinner summer guard hairs begin growing from the same follicles in the skin as the winter hair. The new, growing hair is stronger than the dead winter hair, which has been dried by deep cold. (Almost no moisture exists in sub-freezing mountain air.)

As elk eat the new grass sprouting from the ground, the summer hair grows more quickly, and the old winter hair alongside it begins to slough off. A June elk can look as bedraggled as a 6-year-old boy who's just cut his own hair, but by July the whole herd is almost as sleek as seals in their shorter, finer summer coats.

The summer coat has the same basic coloration as the winter coat—a darker head, neck and legs, and a paler rump patch—but is more reddish. When the winter coat starts coming in during late summer, it's usually lighter in color, giving early fall elk a distinctly orange look. The big bulls turn almost as pale as palomino horses, and across a canyon they can often be seen long before their harems.

The pale rump patch of elk is characteristic of open-country, herding ungulates, allowing members of the herd to be visible to others; it's present but much smaller and has less contrast in the more forest-dwelling red deer. The same relationship can be seen in North America's "New World" deer, mule deer and whitetails. The open-country mule deer has a large dirty-

white rump patch, while the thick-cover whitetail has only a

SUMMER & WINTER COATS

faint white line around its tail (unless, of course, the bright-white underside of the tail is raised in alarm, a short-range method of communication in dim forests). Other open-country ungulates with highly visible rump-patches are prong-horns and bighorn sheep, while moose are typical "patchless" forest animals.

scattered timber, amongst the pines and limestone talus slopes, I've seen bands of a half-dozen bull elk, also brick-red, up to the rounded tips of their short, velvet antlers.

(This same ridge-herding behavior occurs with caribou in the Mulchatna herd of south-central Alaska. On windy or rainy days the caribou utilize habitat anywhere from the rivers to the ridgetops, but if the sun comes out and the wind dies, the herds drift to the open hilltops, letting thermal breezes, caused by sunshine on the hillsides, blow the flies away. One warm late-August day, I sat on a hill and glassed the surrounding ridges, finding swarms of caribou on each open ridgetop with my 10X eyes, clustered as thickly as flies on spilled syrup.)

After their thick winter coats fall away, summer elk wear a sleek, thinner-haired summer coat that is cooler, more dense and protects them from insects.

LOOKING FOR MORE GREEN

*T*his is the time of year when the ex-girlfriend I mentioned in the introduction would see elk everywhere, and wonder what was the big deal with elk hunting. But all that comes to an end in late summer; exactly when depends on rainfall and the amount of grazing.

The lush summer grasses, sedges and forbs grow tougher as they mature—"rank" in the words of old-time range scientists—and also tends to turn toxic, in self-defense from the eager incisors of grazing animals. The big guts of elk can still digest the stuff, but so much extra energy is needed, both to break down tough cellulose and to rid themselves of the increasing poisons, that they don't gain weight.

Elk must put on fat to survive the next winter, so they begin wandering higher in the mountains, following the "green-up line" as winter turns to summer, a thousand feet at a time. Or they drift downhill along streams, grazing on the tender green growth along the water's edge. By summer's end, when the first frosts work their way down the mountains, knocking back the biting insects, elk aren't nearly as concentrated. They can be anywhere from the lowland creeks to the highest tundra meadows.

This toxicity in plants that are grazed or browsed is common in nature. In older growth, the lowest branches and "suckers" of shrubs turn most toxic, because they're in reach of browsing animals like deer and elk. But producing toxins also sucks energy from a plant, so they don't waste this energy growing toxins in branches too high to be browsed. Consequently, higher branches are more edible, which is the reason elk and deer gather around wind-downed or logged trees—and folks who grow trees have to protect the tops of newly planted pines.

It's also the reason that browsing mammals are attracted to new burns, and often grow larger for a few years after a burn. The new growth hasn't had time to develop toxins, so it provides lots of high-quality food. Big burns have provided many such booms in both ruminant numbers and record-book heads. Much of central Idaho was burned during the great forest fires of 1910, and the steep canyons above

the Lochsa and Clearwater and Salmon Rivers were famous for their abundant and large-antlered elk for a human generation, until the browse grew tall again, turning tough and relatively poisonous. The same thing happened after a series of fires early in the 20th century with the moose of Alaska's Kenai Peninsula.

The same thing occurs, to a lesser extent and on a smaller scale, when cattle graze elk range. Studies done at the Boone and Crockett Club's ranch in Montana have shown that grazing during certain times of year by beef cattle can actually improve elk range. Why? Because cows are even bigger than elk, so are able to digest even ranker grass. Their big chompers clear out the tough, thick grass that would otherwise inhibit new growth. When cattle are allowed to graze winter range in late summer, when grass starts to turn rank and then is removed from the range, new grass has a chance to grow up during fall, providing much

A bull elk grazes in late summer, his antlers fully formed and almost ready to lose their velvet. New growth, such as the fresh green of a burn, provides the most abundant minerals for growing antlers.

better food for elk that winter.

Elk, by the way, are more efficient at turning grass into meat than are beef cattle. Most studies indicate that 2.5 elk can grow on the same amount of grass that one cow eats. While elk are smaller than cattle, 2.5 elk (a bull, cow and calf?) have more biomass than one Angus-Hereford cross. Which is why elk "ranchers" can do very well indeed—if they have a market for low-fat wapiti steaks.

LIFE IN SUMMER

To a human culture with a high regard for staying busy, busy, busy during the heat of the day, elk appear very lazy in midsummer. (Not all humanity believes in the heat-hours working day. Some busy Americans are learning the virtues of the siesta, and even many Brits no longer go out in the noonday sun.)

The reason that summer elk lounge around almost constantly is that they're trying to conserve energy for the long winter ahead. Even the nutritious plants of summer aren't nearly as digestible to an elk as meat is to a carnivore. A mouthful of June grass may contain 100 calories, but less than half is digestible, and about half of that is lost through the energy required by digestion. So to gain weight and survive the next winter, elk need to lie around in the summer sun.

Elk calves are weaned relatively slowly. While they can soon start grazing on their own, they do it rather haphazardly, at least to human eyes. Pound-for-pound, calves require relatively more food than their mothers, but don't need to ingest the overall calories of big cows. Calves do need high-quality food, so they pick and choose, wandering here and there to nibble one plant and then another, while summer cows are pretty much eating machines, mowing down

Bull elk appear lazy in late summer, partially for the same reason they appear lazy in mid-winter. They're trying to save energy, putting on fat for the coming rut, and food is so abundant they don't have to move much.

everything in their path.

Calves are often killed by mountain lions during summer because they haven't learned to periodically lift their heads and look around while they feed. This is yet another reason that the more wary cows drift back into selfish herds as soon as possible. And because the cows need to eat more, it's common to see the calves of a herd bunched together near a few watchful cows, while the other cows wander farther as they eat.

Most cows have only one calf. Twins are very rare and, according to one source, occur in no more than one in 300 births, unlike mule and white-tailed deer, which normally have twins and, in years of mild winters and good forage, sometimes triplets.

But the elks' lower birth rate is balanced by the calves' higher survival rate, mostly because elk live in larger herds than deer.

Mule deer tend to herd up more than whitetails, but it's rare to see more than two dozen mule deer together, and these are often family groups on feeding grounds, and the

Elk form larger herds during late summer. Dozens of eyes help protect them from predators while they feed in open meadows.

clan splits up again when they go to bed. But it's very common to see 50 or more elk on a summer range, and occasionally several hundred can be found together in a big mountain basin. Again—the selfish herd promotes survival, especially of the calves that make it through their first month.

ELK TALK

The new calves learn to communicate quickly with their mothers. Calves and cows talk to each other a lot, each letting the other know where they are, even in a close-knit herd, especially when bedded in shady timber where the animals can't always see each other. The main calf call is a higher-pitched version of the mature elk's "meow," and unless the calf grows frightened, its call is normally less drawn-out than that of a cow. When a calf is really scared, its calls become almost painful to human ears, sometimes sounding almost like the shrieks and screams of human children.

But the normal everyday talk of a cow-calf herd is made up of short squeals and meows and chirps that sound remarkably like some bird calls. Herds don't talk constantly, since steady noise might attract predators (including humans). Instead, the elk will be lying around or feeding silently when suddenly a cow misses her calf, or a calf spooks a magpie out of the grass and gives a short squeal. The whole herd then erupts into arrhythmic song—meows, squeals and chirps wafting back and forth on the warm air for 10 or 20 seconds until everybody's satisfied.

The worst elk sound a hunter can hear is their alarm bark, which to me sounds remarkably like that of a red fox—except louder, of course, since an average cow is about 50 times the size of an average fox. In timber, a crescendo of barks normally fades into

A cow-calf herd keeps in contact with each other through short chirps and squeals. But they don't talk constantly, because too much noise would attract predators.

the thumping of tree trunks and breaking of branches as the herd takes off at a full run. There are some African animals that can make more noise running off through trees—giraffes and elephants immediately come to mind—but a dozen elk can make you think 100 wild longhorn bulls have been let loose in the lodgepole.

On opening day of my first bow season many years ago, I parked my Bronco at the gate of a closed logging road on the northwest side of a long ridge above Ninemile Creek outside Missoula, Montana. The closed road wandered through heavy timber at about the same elevation along the ridge, crossing the heads of several small creeks. This was just the sort of place an elk herd would probably be in early September, so with high hopes I strung my recurve and placed a diaphragm call between my front teeth, ready for action.

Then I closed the door of the Bronco. What sounded like a whole sackfull of foxes started barking in the nearby timber. Then the trees shook briefly, and I heard a scatter of dull thumps like a dozen ostrich eggs falling onto a football field, mixed with the crack of broken branches. The timber went silent, and I tiptoed over there, call in my mouth and arrow nocked. I could smell where they'd been, a smell like a June cattle pasture, and soon found hoofprints in the slightly damp earth. But the elk, of course, were long gone. So I shrugged and hiked four miles along that road, cow-calling into every cool canyon, and never heard a peep or saw a fresh elk track on the soft shoulders of the road. Finally I hiked back, finding one blue grouse near the locked gate, which I missed. Those were the only damn elk on that whole mountainside.

Early fall is the time of the bowhunter, who attempts to enter the elk's world undetected by their eyes, noses and ears. It doesn't work very often, but just coming close is often enough.

AN END ‡ A BEGINNING

All of this is pretty typical of late-summer elk. Once the big-meadow grass turns tough and awful-tasting, the big cow-calf herds break up into family units and scatter. They can be anywhere, even right next to a locked gate. Such smaller herds are more able to feed on smaller openings in timber, where plants remain green thanks to a lower evaporation rate, and more palatable because they haven't been grazed as much. Several studies have shown that late-summer elk tend to eat more forbs than grasses and sedges.

Late-summer elk are not as visible as elk on windblown January ridges, or cows and calves scattered across a green June hilltop in the breeze above the flies. But by this time of year, both bulls and cows are feeling a sense of restlessness.

The herds of cows and calves can be seen wandering along the edges of big clearings, poking their noses down into the summer-dried grass to pluck the leaves of lupine. The calves have learned to lift their heads and look around the meadow, and the herd seems to fit the landscape better, their paler autumn coats beginning to dull the brick-red of summer hair. Instead of either the bright contrast of red elk against green June wheatgrass, or the scatter of elk like black ants against a distant January ridge, elk in the last few weeks before the autumnal equinox seem to meld into their landscape, almost like the figures in an impressionistic painting.

The colors of the meadows and rough conifer trunks and elk are all just slightly different, the spectrum of tans and oranges and dark browns

As fall approaches elk become restless for a couple of reasons. First, their forage is changing with the dry weather of late summer and the first frosts. Plus, their winter coats are growing, forcing elk out of sunny meadows and into shady timber.

forming a natural composition, painted by somebody with a more subtle sense of color than any camera. And a certain alertness in the elk adds emotion to the painting: They are obviously waiting for something to happen.

The bulls, of course, have extra testosterone running through their arteries, into their antlers and testicles and brains. But even the cows feel some undercurrent in the cooling mountain air. When they wake in the predawn of late August, they often find the grass brittle with frost, and on one of those hard cold mornings the belly-deep roar and whistle of a suddenly lonely bull will be heard along a blue ridge, like an early prediction of snow. And in the few seconds it takes his high thin call to reach the other side of the valley, last year finds this year, and the circle begins to turn within itself once more. ✖

Late summer turns to early autumn, and another season of renewal begins.

Bibliography

Bugle magazine. Missoula, Montana: The Rocky Mountain Elk Foundation.

Chase, Alston. *Playing God In Yellowstone*. New York, New York: Harcourt Brace Jovanovich Publishers, 1987.

Geist, Valerius. *Elk Country*. Minocqua, Wisconsin: NorthWord Press, 1991.

Geist, Valerius. *Deer of the World*. Mechanicsburg, Pennsylvania: Stackpole Books, 1998.

Jennings, Jesse D. *Prehistory of North America*. New York, New York: McGraw-Hill Book Company, 1968.

Karwaski, Lorraine (editor). *Montana Big Game Trophies, 10th Edition*. Helena, Montana: Montana Department of Fish, Wildlife & Parks, 1996.

Keith, Elmer. *Hell, I Was There!* Los Angeles, California: Petersen Publishing Co., 1979.

Laubach, Don and Mark Henckel. *Elk Talk*. Helena, Montana: Falcon Press, 1987.

Montana Department of Fish, Wildlife & Parks. *Antlered Elk and Deer Management in Montana*. Helena, Montana, 1985.

Murie, Margaret and Olaus. *Wapiti Wilderness*. New York, New York: Alfred A. Knopf, 1966.

Spomer, Ron. *The Rut*. Minocqua, Wisconsin: Willow Creek Press, 1996.

Reneau, Jack and Susan C. (editors). *Records of North American Big Game, 10th Edition*. Missoula, Montana: The Boone and Crockett Club, 1993.

Russell, Osborne. *Journal Of A Trapper*. Lincoln, Nebraska: University of Nebraska Press, 1965.

Thwaites, Reuben Gold. *Original Journals of the Lewis and Clark Expedition*. Arno Press reprint of the 1904 Dodd, Mead & Company edition.

Thomas, Jack Ward and Dale E. Toweill (editors). *Elk of North America, Ecology and Management*. Harrisburg, Pennsylvania: Stackpole Books, 1982.

Whitehead, G. Kenneth. *The Whitehead Encylclopedia of Deer*. Shrewsbury, England: Swan Hill Press, 1993.